A YIDDISH HAMLET

Borgo Press Books by FRANK J. MORLOCK

Castor and Pollux and Other Opera Libretti (Editor)
The Chevalier d'Éon and Other Short Farces (Editor)
Chuzzlewit
Congreve's Comedy of Manners
Crime and Punishment
Cyrano and Molière: Five Plays by or About Molière (Editor)
Doctor Scratch and Other Plays (Editor)
Falstaff (with Shakespeare, John Dennis, & William Kendrick)
Fathers and Sons
Herculaneum & Sardanapalus: Two Opera Libretti (Editor)
The Idiot
Isle of Slaves and Other Plays (Editor)
Jurgen
Justine
The Londoners & The Green Carnation: Two Plays
Lord Jim
The Madwoman of Beresina & Other Napoleonic Plays (Editor)
Notes from the Underground
Oblomov
Old Creole Days
Outrageous Women: Lady Macbeth and Other Plays (Editor)
Peter and Alexis
The Princess Casamassima
A Raw Youth
Salammbô & Dido: Two Operas (Editor)
The Stendhal Hamlet Scenarios and Other Shakespearean Shorts from the French (Editor)
Two Voltairean Plays: The Triumvirate; Comedy at Ferney
Whitewashing Julia and Other Plays
The Widow's Husband; and, Porthos in Search of an Outfit: Two Dumasian Comedies (Editor)
A Yiddish Hamlet and Other Plays
Zeneida & The Follies of Love & The Cat Who Changed into a Woman: Two Plays (Editor)

A YIDDISH HAMLET

AND OTHER PLAYS

FRANK J. MORLOCK

THE BORGO PRESS
MMXIII

A YIDDISH HAMLET

Copyright © 1982, 1986, 2013 by Frank J. Morlock

FIRST EDITION

Published by Wildside Press LLC

www.wildsidebooks.com

DEDICATION

To My Dear Friends,
Dan and Donna Woloshen

CONTENTS

A YIDDISH HAMLET, adapted from a story by Israel
Zangwill. 9
CAST OF CHARACTERS. 10
ACT I. 11
ACT II 25
ACT III 44
ACT IV 52
ACT V 63
THE CONGRESSMAN'S NIGHTMARE 71
CAST OF CHARACTERS. 72
THE PLAY 73
THE MOONSHINE VINE 141
CAST OF CHARACTERS. 142
THE PLAY 143
ABOUT THE AUTHOR 211

A YIDDISH HAMLET
ADAPTED FROM A STORY BY ISRAEL ZANGWILL

CAST OF CHARACTERS

M. PINCHAS, a Yiddish poet

OSTROVSKY, a Yiddish playwright

SCHNEEMAN, his toady

TUCH

WITBERG, a violinist

VON MIESES, another poet, also Horatio

HEATHEN JOURNALIST, also Polonius

GRUNBITZ

GOLDWATER, an actor manager, also Hamlet

KLOOT, his factotum

CHARACTERS IN THE HAMLET PLAY:

THE QUEEN

OPHELIA (Mrs. Goldwater)

ACT I

An East Side café at the turn of the century—daytime.

The customers are almost exclusively Jewish except for the Heathen Journalist. Many are dressed in traditional costumes, with black hats, black clothes and long beards. Grunbitz, Tuch, and the Heathen Journalist are seated at a large table, awaiting the arrival of Pinchas. Schneeman and Ostrovsky sit nearby at another table.

SCHNEEMAN

He's coming, this seven-day wonder.

OSTROVSKY (bitterly)

They do nothing but talk about this fool poet from Warsaw. They forget Ostrovsky overnight. Fifty-three plays I've written, fifty-three.

SCHNEEMAN

They'll forget him overnight, too. This "Yiddish Hamlet" is sure to flop.

OSTROVSKY

Who knows? The public is fickle.

(Pinchas enters, escorted by Witberg and Von Mieses, who lead him very deferentially to the table at which the Heathen Journalist, Tuch, and Grunbitz are waiting. Pinchas is greeted and congratulated by all and begins to hold forth.)

PINCHAS

It is the greatest play of the generation. (complacently) It will be translated into every tongue.

OSTROVSKY

Will you listen to that conceited ass? Wait till Goldwater gets through rewriting it.

SCHNEEMAN

I can't wait to see Goldwater squeeze his fat carcass into a pair of tights to play "Hamlet".

PINCHAS

I, Melchitzedek Pinchas, will soon be world-famous. See, my initials M. P. make Master Playwright.

OSTROVSKY (to Schneeman)

Also Mud Pusher. Who is this uncombed bunco artist?

SCHNEEMAN

He calls himself the sweet singer of Israel.

TUCH (to Pinchas)

But look here, Pinchas. You said the other day your initials made Messianic Poet.

PINCHAS

And don't they? You call yourself a ward boss, a political leader, and statesman and you don't know your ABC's.

(There is a roar of laughter at this sally.)

TUCH (nettled)

They can't stand for everything.

PINCHAS

No, they can't stand for mad politician. (another burst of laughter) But, as there are many meanings in every letter of the Torah, so there are meanings innumerable in every letter of my name. (ingenuously) If I am a playwright as well as a poet, was not Shakespeare also?

TUCH (sarcastic but not ill-natured)

You wouldn't class yourself with that low-down barnstormer?

PINCHAS (modestly)

My superiority to Shakespeare I leave for others to discover. I discovered it for myself in writing this very play, but I cannot expect the world to admit it until the play is produced.

WITBERG (innocently)

How did you come to find it out yourself?

PINCHAS

It happened quite naturally. You see when Goldwater was touring with his Yiddish troupe through London, he had the idea of acquainting the Jewish masses with Hamlet, and he asked me to make the Yiddish translation, as one great poet translating another. Well, I started the job and then, of course, the discovery was inevitable.

TUCH (drily)

Doubtless.

PINCHAS (munching on some food which he brandishes from time to time)

The play, which I had not read since my youth, appeared unspeakably childish in places. (brandishing) Take for example the ghost. (munches, then slightly annoyed) This bagel is as stale as a sermon. Command me a cream tart, Witberg. (Witberg goes to a waiter) (resuming) What was I saying?

TUCH

The ghost—

PINCHAS

As yes...now, how can a ghost impress a modern audience which no longer believes in ghosts?

TUCH

That is true.

PINCHAS (sensing approbation, waves his index finger, then presses it on the side of his nose)

I translated Shakespeare, yes. But into modern terms. The ghost vanished. Hamlet's tragedy remained only the incapacity of the thinker for the base activity of action.

OSTROVSKY

The higher activity, you mean.

TUCH

Thought has no value until it is translated into action.

SCHNEEMAN

Exactly, you've got to work it up.

PINCHAS

Schtuss! Acts are but the soldiers. Thought is the general.

WITBERG (having returned with a cream tart)

It is not much use thinking about playing the violin, Pinchas.

PINCHAS

You performers are all alike. Every tune you play, every word in the mouth of an actor, was put there by someone else. (waving his arms) Yet you think you are indispensable!

WITBERG

Well, someone has to perform it, in order to test your ideas.

PINCHAS

No doubt the leading man who plays my Hamlet will think he is more important than the playwright. Woe be to the mummer that dares tamper with a single syllable.

OSTROVSKY

Your Hamlet! Since when?

PINCHAS

Since I recreated him for the modern world without tinsel and pasteboard; since I conceived him in fire and bore him in agony; since... (biting into his cream tart and making a face) even this cream tart is sour!—since I carried him to and fro in my pocket as a young kangaroo in the pouch of its mother.

HEATHEN JOURNALIST

Why didn't Iselmann produce it in London?

PINCHAS

Because of the ghost. (disgusted) I have changed Iselmann's name to Eselmann, the donkey man. I had hardly read him ten lines before he brayed out, "Where is the ghost?" I said, "I have laid him. He cannot walk on the modern stage." Eselmann tore his hair. "But it is for the ghost that I was interested. Yiddish audiences love a ghost." "They love your acting, too," I replied. He failed to comprehend the withering irony of that retort. Oh, I gave that donkey man a piece of my mind.

GRUNBITZ (jesting)

But he didn't take a piece.

PINCHAS

As if a great poet were to consider the tastes of the mob. Bah! These managers are all men of the earth. Crass materialists. (rising)

Once, in my days of obscurity, I was made to put a bosom into a play, and it swept all my genius off the boards. But I am glad Eselmann gave me my Hamlet back, for, before giving it to Goldwater, I made it even more subtle. No vulgar nonsense of fencing and poison at the end...a pure mental tragedy, for in life it is the soul alone that counts. My play is the eternal tragedy of the thinker. (turning to Witberg) Another bagel.

(Witberg goes in search of a waiter.)

HEATHEN JOURNALIST

Strikes me, Pin'cuss, you're giving us Hamlet without the Prince of Denmark.

PINCHAS

Better than the Prince of Denmark without Hamlet, as he is usually played. In my version the Prince of Denmark indeed vanishes, for Hamlet is a Jew and the Prince of Palestine.

(General consternation in the café.)

VON MIESES

You have made him a Jew?

PINCHAS

If he is to be the ideal thinker, let him belong to a nation of thinkers. In fact, (confidentially) the play is virtually an autobiography.

HEATHEN JOURNALIST

You still call it Hamlet?

PINCHAS

Why not? True, it is virtually a new work and vastly superior to the original. But Shakespeare borrowed his story from an older play and treated it to suit himself; why, therefore, should I not treat Shakespeare as it suits me?

HEATHEN JOURNALIST

But wouldn't it be better to modify the title so people don't get confused?

PINCHAS

If I were to call it by another name, some learned fool would pretend it was stolen from Shakespeare; this way it challenges comparison.

TUCH (drily)

And Shakespeare suffers.

PINCHAS (placidly)

Only as a medieval alchemist or astrologer suffers in comparison with a modern chemist or astronomer. The muddle-headedness of Shakespeare—which incidentally is the cause of the muddle in Hamlet's character—has given way to the clear vision of the modern. How could Shakespeare describe a thinker? The Elizabethans could not think. They were like our politicians.

GRUNBITZ

Why should you expect thought from a politician? (Tuch looks angry) That's like expecting money from an economist. Besides, only youth thinks.

PINCHAS

That is well said. He who is ever thinking never grows old. I shall die young like all those whom the gods love. Waiter, give Mr. Grunbitz a cup of chocolate and a cream tart.

GRUNBITZ

Thank you...no.

PINCHAS

You cannot refuse. You will pain Witberg, who is paying.

VON MIESES (embarrassed)

I wonder if you could look at these poems.

PINCHAS (graciously)

I'll be glad to give you my opinion, but I warn you I am a severe critic.

OSTROVSKY (to Schneeman)

Ohh! He's a critic too.

SCHNEEMAN (to Ostrovsky)

What a pompous ass.

OSTROVSKY

Do you suppose he has any talent at all?

SCHNEEMAN

He's a Yiddish Bernard Shaw, no doubt. (laughing) Wait till Goldwater gets through with him.

PINCHAS (who has been perusing Mieses' poems joyfully)

But it is full of genius! I might have written it myself. The third stanza is a masterpiece.

VON MIESES

Perhaps I, too, shall write a play one day. My initial 'M' makes master too.

PINCHAS (graciously)

It may be that you are destined to wear my mantle.

(Mieses looks uneasily at Pinchas' ill-fitting and ragged cloak.)

PINCHAS

And now, Mieses, you must give me carfare. I have to go and

talk to Goldwater about rehearsals. That pumpkin-head of an actor-manager is capable of any crime. Even altering my best lines.

OSTROVSKY (maliciously)

I suppose Goldwater plays Hamlet.

PINCHAS (airily)

We have not discussed it yet.

OSTROVSKY

He'll be all right. So long as Fanny Goldwater doesn't play Ophelia.

PINCHAS

Mrs. Goldwater play Ophelia? She wouldn't dare! Don't dream of such a thing. She belongs in vaudeville.

OSTROVSKY

All right. Don't say I didn't warn you.

PINCHAS (shaken)

You don't think there is really a danger?

OSTROVSKY

He usually gives her the best female role.

PINCHAS (venomously)

I'll drown her before I let her play my Ophelia.

OSTROVSKY (coolly)

Well, it's up to you.

PINCHAS (shaking his fist)

The minx. But I'll manage her. If worse comes to worst. I'll make love to her.

(The café erupts in laughter at this threat.)

TUCH

And when is the grand event? When will it open?

PINCHAS

After Passover. (buttoning his coat) I'd better get going before he casts her as Ophelia. (sarcastically) I don't want her to be disappointed.

OSTROVSKY

Has Goldwater given you a contract?

PINCHAS (with great dignity and disdain)

I am a poet, not a lawyer. Parchments are for merchants; honest men build on the word.

OSTROVSKY

It comes to the same thing. These managers can slip out of any contract. Still, I prefer to force them to use their imagination by getting it in writing. When I'm not writing plays, I'm busy writing contracts. It prevents writer's block. (with great deliberation) I will come to your opening night.

PINCHAS

It will be a tribute which the audience will appreciate. Wait till you see my play. You must all come. I will send you all boxes. Then you will learn that thought is greater than action. Thought is the greatest thing in the world!

(Pinchas and Witberg leave. Ostrovsky puffs his cigar, then he rises and goes to a phone.)

OSTROVSKY

Is that you, Goldwater? Yes, I'm fine. No, it's not about the money you owe me. Purely artistic. I wanted to tell you that I look forward to seeing you as Hamlet and your missus as Ophelia.

(pause)

Hadn't thought of her as Ophelia? Goldwater, you must be losing all your artistic sense.

(pause)

Of course, she'll be perfect. By the way, that wild man who wrote the play is on his way over there to see you. Better dodge him. After all, you shouldn't let the author ruin the play—

(facing the audience)

—when you can do it yourself.

(pause)

By the way, now you mention the money...

(he looks at the receiver which has gone dead)

I should have known....

(Ostrovsky hangs up, smiles, puffs his cigar, and resumes his seat contentedly. He looks at a newspaper.)

BLACKOUT

ACT II

The dressing room of Goldwater's Yiddish Theater, daytime.

Goldwater is applying his makeup; Kloot, his brash young assistant is sitting on the table. There are sounds of a scuffle outside.

PINCHAS

(forcing his way in)

Not thus. Not thus shall you treat my Hamlet. Every syllable must be engraved upon the actors' hearts, or God forbid the curtain to go up. Not that it matters, with the foolish play you are now butchering; it is ink vomit, not literature.

(Goldwater is ignoring him and angrily changing his trousers. Kloot remains impassive.)

GOLDWATER

Son of a witch! You come and disturb all my house. What do you want?

PINCHAS

I want to talk to you about rehearsals.

GOLDWATER

(placatingly)

I told you I would let you know when rehearsals begin.

PINCHAS

But you forgot to take my address.

GOLDWATER

As if I don't know where to find you!

KLOOT

Pinchas gets drinks from the whole café.

PINCHAS

They drink to the health of Hamlet.

GOLDWATER

All right: Kloot, get his address. Good evening.

PINCHAS

But when will it be? I must know.

GOLDWATER

(patiently)

We can't fix it to a day. There's plenty of money in this play yet.

PINCHAS

Money...bah! But merit?

GOLDWATER

You authors are jealous as the devil.

PINCHAS

Me! Jealous of donkeys? In Central Park you see giraffes and tortoises too. Central Park has more talent than this scribbler of yours.

GOLDWATER

Ostrovsky wrote it and he's very popular.

PINCHAS

Ostrovsky...a pygmy talent. He uses all kinds of American slang. His Yiddish is not pure. His locutions odious. Not to mention the fact he can't write.

KLOOT

I'll write you about rehearsals.

PINCHAS

But I must know weeks ahead. I may go lecturing. The great continent calls for me. In Chicago, in Cincinnati....

GOLDWATER

Don't trouble yourself. Make your own plans and go. We know

how to put on a play. We can do without you.

PINCHAS

Do without me? A nice mess you will make of it! I must instruct you how to say every line.

GOLDWATER

(astonished)

You, instruct me?

PINCHAS

(realizing that Goldwater is not be trifled with on this point)

I, I don't mean you personally. I mean the company. I will show them the accent, the gesture. I'm a great stage manager as well as a great poet. The 'M' in my name makes manager. There shall be no more prompter.

GOLDWATER

Indeed. And how are you going to get on without a prompter?

PINCHAS

Very simple. A month's rehearsal.

GOLDWATER

(drily)

We usually get by with a week's rehearsal.

KLOOT

(ironically)

It is very good of you to give us a month of your valuable time.

GOLDWATER

(irate)

A month! I could put on six melodramas in a month.

PINCHAS

(shocked)

But Hamlet is not a melodrama.

GOLDWATER

(imperturbably)

Quite so. That's why it's so easy. There is not half the scenery. It's the scenery that takes time rehearsing, not the dialogue.

PINCHAS

(enraged)

You would profane my divine work by gabbling through it with your pack of geese parroting the prompter!

KLOOT

You just come down a peg or two. You do the writing, we do the rest.

PINCHAS

(imperiously)

Silence, impudent face! You are not talking to Ostrovsky. I am a poet and I demand my rights.

(Kloot and Goldwater are astounded by his impudence.)

GOLDWATER

(recovering)

What rights? I paid you twenty dollars and that was too much.

PINCHAS

Twenty dollars? For the masterpiece of the twentieth century?

KLOOT

In the twenty-first century you shall have twenty-five dollars.

PINCHAS

(superbly)

Make mock as you please. I shall be living in the fifty-first century even. Poets never die although, alas, they have to live. Twenty dollars too much indeed! It is not a dollar a century for the run of the play.

GOLDWATER

(pacing a bit, then grimly)

Very well. Give those twenty dollars back. We return your play.

PINCHAS

(confused)

No, no, Goldwater...I must not disappoint my printer. I have promised him twenty dollars to print my Hebrew "Selections from Nietzsche."

GOLDWATER

(implacably)

You take your manuscript and give me my money.

PINCHAS

(desperately)

Exchange would be a robbing. I will not rob you. Keep your bargain. See. Here's the printer's letter.

(Pinchas rummages excitedly in his pockets and drags forth letters and manuscripts from his overcoat. Goldwater waives a repudiating hand.)

Be not a fool, man. Goldwater, I and you are the only two people in New York who serve the poetic drama. I, by writing, you by producing.

(Goldwater still shakes his head, but less vigorously. The flattery is appeasing him.)

KLOOT

Your manuscript will be returned to you by the next garbage truck.

PINCHAS

(disregarding Kloot)

I have faith in you, Goldwater. I am willing you shall have only a fortnight's rehearsals.

(trying harder)

I have always said the only genius of the Yiddish stage is Goldwater. Klosterman—bah! He's not a bad producer, but act? My grandmother's hen has a better stage presence. And there is Davidoff—a voice like a frog and a walk like a spider. And these charlatans I only heard of when I came to New York. But you, Goldwater—your fame has blown across the Atlantic. I journeyed from Poland expressly to collaborate with you.

GOLDWATER

(mollified)

Then why do you spoil it all?

PINCHAS

It is my anxiety that Europe shall not be disappointed in you. Let us talk of the cast.

GOLDWATER

It's too early yet.

PINCHAS

The early bird catches the worm.

KLOOT

But all our worms are caught. We keep them penned up on the premises.

PINCHAS

(aghast)

I know, I know.

GOLDWATER

But we don't give all our talent to one play.

PINCHAS

(breathing a breath of hope)

No, of course not.

GOLDWATER

We have to use all our people by turns. We divide our forces. With myself as Hamlet, you will have a cast that should satisfy any author, even the bard himself.

PINCHAS

(with wonderful hypocrisy)

Do I not know it? Were you but to say your lines, leaving all the others to be read by the prompter, the audience would be spellbound.

GOLDWATER

That being so, you have no right to expect to have my wife in the same cast.

PINCHAS

No, indeed. Two such geniuses in the same cast would be beyond all expectation, like the sun and the moon shining together.

(Pinchas is really getting carried away)

Besides, Ophelia is such a small part. She deserves the part of Hamlet to really show her talent.

GOLDWATER

Heaven forbid my wife should appear in breeches. She would never so lower herself.

PINCHAS

(complacently)

That is what makes it impossible for her to appear in the play.

GOLDWATER

But, you lucky man, the impossible has happened. Fanny has decided to sacrifice herself. Two Goldwaters in the cast. Think of it.

PINCHAS

Who am I that I should ask her to sacrifice herself?

KLOOT

Fanny won't sacrifice Ophelia.

PINCHAS

(aside, between his teeth)

She'll execute her.

GOLDWATER

(fortunately not hearing)

You hear? My wife will not sacrifice Ophelia, by leaving her to a minor player. She thinks only of the play.

PINCHAS

(disconcerted, but still trying to be polite)

It is very noble of her. But she worked so hard lately. She must need a rest, a vacation. It is such a trying part.

GOLDWATER

My wife never spares herself.

PINCHAS

(losing his head)

But she might spare Ophelia.

GOLDWATER

(gruffly)

What do you mean? My wife will honor you by playing Ophelia.

(with a wave of his hand)

That is ended.

PINCHAS

(wildly)

No, it is not ended. Your wife is a comedienne, not a tragedienne.

GOLDWATER

(puzzled)

You yourself just called her a genius.

PINCHAS

For comedy. For comedy, I will allow. But Hamlet is not a comedy. Your wife prances, skips, and jumps. Rather would I give Ophelia to a kangaroo or jackrabbit!

GOLDWATER

(indignant)

Swine! Compare my wife to a kangaroo or jackrabbit! Take

your filthy manuscript and begone....

KLOOT

(to himself)

Well, Fanny would provide an element of comic relief! Hey, that's an idea.

PINCHAS

To gratify your wife, you would make her ridiculous and deprive the world of your Hamlet!

GOLDWATER

I can get plenty of Hamlets. Any scribbler can translate Shakespeare.

PINCHAS

(sublimely)

Surely, you can get hundreds. But who can surpass Shakespeare? Who can make him intelligible to the modern soul?

(Goldwater hesitates, thinking perhaps there is something to it.)

A VOICE FROM OFFSTAGE

Mr. Goldwater, your cue.

(Goldwater rushes out, glad to escape.)

PINCHAS

(pleading)

You will talk to him, Kloot? You will save Ophelia?

KLOOT

(easily)

Rely on me, if I have to play her myself.

PINCHAS

(worriedly)

But that will be even worse.

KLOOT

How do you know? You've never seen me act. I'm a great female impersonator.

PINCHAS

(soothing, wheedling)

You will not spoil my play. You will get me a maidenly Ophelia. I and you are the only two men in New York who understand how to cast a play.

KLOOT

You leave it to me. I have a wife of my own.

PINCHAS

(alarmed)

What! Don't you dare.

KLOOT

Don't be alarmed. I'll coach her. She's just the age for the part. Mrs. Goldwater could be her mother.

PINCHAS

But can she make an audience cry?

KLOOT

You bet. A regular onion of an Ophelia.

PINCHAS

But I must see her rehearse, then I decide.

KLOOT

Of course.

PINCHAS

And you will seek me in the café when rehearsals begin?

KLOOT

That goes without saying. How can we rehearse without you? You shouldn't have worried the boss. We'll call you even if it's the middle of the night.

(Pinchas jumps at Kloot and kisses him on both cheeks.)

PINCHAS

Protector of Poets!

(releasing him)

And you will see that they do not mutilate my play? You will not suffer a single hair of my poesy to be harmed?

KLOOT

Not a hair shall be cut.

PINCHAS

Ahhh, I and you are the only two men in New York who know how to treat poetry.

(hugging Kloot again)

KLOOT

You bet.

(escaping from Pinchas)

Well, goodbye.

PINCHAS

(still not convinced)

And you will see it is not adulterated with American slang? In Zion they don't say 'sure' and 'lend me a nickel.'

KLOOT

Didn't I promise? Don't you trust me?

PINCHAS

All the same, you might lend me a nickel for carfare.

KLOOT

I'd be honored.

PINCHAS

Goodbye, my protector.

(he goes out)

KLOOT

That was a nickel well spent.

(The door opens again, Pinchas' ungainly head reappearing.)

PINCHAS

You promise me all this?

KLOOT

(trying to appear hurt)

Didn't I do it already?

PINCHAS

Save a poet from distraction and swear to me.

KLOOT

Will you go if I swear?

PINCHAS

Yup.

KLOOT

And you won't come back again till rehearsals begin?

PINCHAS

Nup.

KLOOT

Then I swear on my father and mother's life.

PINCHAS

(grinning, satisfied at last)

Thank you! I'm going.

(he leaves, closing the door behind him)

KLOOT

(locks and bolts the door)

I wonder how he'd feel if he knew I'm an orphan? Sure was a good thing we didn't tell him we plan to add music.

(Kloot goes out whistling)

BLACKOUT

ACT III

The East Side Café, night.

It is the evening of Opening Night. Most of the persons present in the first scene are in the café, but there is no center of attention. Enter Pinchas tumultuously. Striding up and down, brandishing his cane in one hand and a poster in the other, Pinchas is nearly frothing at the mouth.

OSTROVSKY

(reading the poster)

"Itzek Goldberg proudly presents the Yiddish Hamlet, by the world-renowned poet Melchitzedek Pinchas, with music by Ignatz Levitsky, the world-famous composer. Starring Itzek Goldberg and the world-acclaimed Fanny Goldberg."

(maliciously)

What seems to be the matter?

PINCHAS

The matter! The matter! World-famous composer, indeed. Whoever heard of Ignatz Levitsky? And who wants his music? The tragedy of a thinker needs no caterwauling of violins. Does

Goldwater imagine I have written a melodrama? At most I will permit an overture.

OSTROVSKY

Whoever heard of Melchitzedek Pinchas? World-famous author. That's rich.

PINCHAS

(not hearing him)

The dogs. The liars.

WITBERG

(trying to placate him)

Perhaps a little well-placed music would not hurt.

PINCHAS

They won't even let me attend rehearsals. Who can tell how they have mangled it? Such ghouls.

TUCH

After all, Goldberg knows his business.

VON MIESES

You shouldn't have tried to replace Fanny. Goldberg is very proud of his wife's talent.

PINCHAS

He has reason. She has so little, every bit is precious.

OSTROVSKY

(rubbing it in)

Where are our tickets? You promised us all box seats.

PINCHAS

They didn't send me any. Liars. Murderers. Slayers of poets. They fear I fire Ophelia.

OSTROVSKY

(relishing his rival's predicament, especially as he has suffered the same fate himself)

Surely you are going to attend?

PINCHAS

(dejected)

The box office is sold out.

OSTROVSKY

Well, that's a good sign.

PINCHAS

I don't believe them. It's a conspiracy to keep me out. But they won't succeed.

TUCH

What will you do?

PINCHAS

(raving)

I'll do something, if I have to fire the theatre.

OSTROVSKY

Why don't you call Goldwater on the phone?

PINCHAS

That's an excellent idea. Will I give him a piece of my mind. Witberg, a dime.

(Taking a dime from Witberg, he strides to the phone, followed by the whole café, eager to hear some precious witticisms.)

OSTROVSKY

Be sure to disguise your voice.

(Pinchas dials and waits.)

TUCH

This will go down in history.

MIESES

It may not be a good idea.

PINCHAS

(in a high-pitched voice)

This is George Bernard Shaw, you Goldwater? May I speak to Goldwater, tell him the critic Bernard Shaw wants to congratulate him.

(to the crowd)

Goldwater's too dumb to know that Shaw doesn't speak Yiddish.

(in a high-pitched voice)

Hello, Mr. Goldwater, is that you? It is.

(changing back to his natural voice)

Pigs! Pigs! Pigs! You and Kloot. I have cast my pearls before swine. May a sudden death smite you. May the curtain fall on you, you gibbering epileptic baboon. What do you mean you can't hear? Speak plainer? I will speak plainer, swineherd! Never again shall a work of mine defile itself in your dirty dollar factory. I spit on you. Phutt....

(spitting into the receiver)

Your father was a Meshummad and your mother.... Don't hang up, I'm not finished.... And your mother, an Irish fish wife.

(turning from the phone)

He hung up. Coward. I had a lot more to say. That was worth ten cents.

(He hangs up the phone and walks to a table with great satisfaction.)

OSTROVSKY

I'll say this for him. He's got shtick. The happiest day in my life would be to say half of what he just said to Goldwater.

(Enter Heathen Journalist.)

HEATHEN JOURNALIST

Congratulations, Pin'cuss. Your play's a great success.

PINCHAS

Ehh?

HEATHEN JOURNALIST

I had to leave early; got a deadline to meet. Nearly eleven and only two acts finished. You'll have to brisk 'em up a bit.

PINCHAS

If I get my hands on Goldwater, I'll brisk him up. Never fear.

(uneasily)

How was the play?

HEATHEN JOURNALIST

Well, it's not quite what I expected from listening to you, or reading Shakespeare. All that cabaret music and those funny lines.

PINCHAS

Cabaret music! Funny lines! There wasn't a funny line in the whole play.

HEATHEN JOURNALIST

There is now. Mrs. Goldwater is stealing the show, she's a howling success.

PINCHAS

(ready to weep)

Howling success. I'll kill them. All of them.

HEATHEN JOURNALIST

Well, got to go. Congrats.

(The Heathen Journalist starts for the door, but suddenly Pinchas gives chase.)

PINCHAS

Still got your theatre ticket?

HEATHEN JOURNALIST

What for?

PINCHAS

Give it to me. With that I can get in.

HEATHEN JOURNALIST

Sure, take it.

(He gives the ticket to Pinchas, who rushes out, yelling, "Now, Goldwater".)

OSTROVSKY

(to the Journalist)

You may just have become an accessory to murder.

HEATHEN JOURNALIST

Hey, would that make a headline. 'Poet slays leading man.' I better go and see.

(he rushes out after Pinchas)

OSTROVSKY

What about your deadline?

HEATHEN JOURNALIST

It can wait.

(They all stare after Pinchas and the Journalist.)

BLACKOUT

ACT IV

Goldwater's Jewish Theatre, daytime.

We are at a slightly different perspective. We can see the stage in the background, looking from the wings. Hamlet is with his Mother.

QUEEN

"I made you some nice food. You should eat something. You never eat, that's why you have these morbid ideas."

HAMLET

"I must meet this specter on the ramparts."

QUEEN

"You should look out for the ghost. I don't want you getting hurt. Besides it's very damp tonight. If you must go, you should wear your galoshes."

(Hamlet/Goldwater exits to where Kloot is standing in the wings, observing.)

QUEEN

"That kid never listened to his mother. Never."

(Loud applause, whistles, etc.)

GOLDWATER

They're loving it, Kloot. They're swallowing it like ice cream soda.

(The Hamlet play continues in mime. We cannot hear what they are saying but the audience in Goldwater's theatre can, and they titter, roar, and laugh. Ophelia enters, a buxom, comical woman, and pirouettes to applause. She carries a Palm Branch and shakes it to every point in the compass. Thunderous applause.)

GOLDWATER

This Pinchas is a genius after all.

KLOOT

We got our money's worth.

GOLDWATER

Next I'm going to commission Pinchas to adapt Macbeth. Don't you think Fanny would make a fantastic Lady Macbeth?

KLOOT

I see her more as Desdemona.

GOLDWATER

A genius. That's what you are. A genius.

KLOOT

(modestly)

I know it.

(Pinchas is seen stealthily approaching along the wall.)

KLOOT

That's your cue.

(Goldwater returns to greet the ghost, a figure in a white sheet that cakewalks across the stage. Pinchas tries to bound onto the stage shouting "Villains," but Kloot has seen him and collars him in an iron grip.)

KLOOT

(unruffled)

You don't take your call yet.

PINCHAS

(in a fury)

Let me go. I must speak to the people. They think me, Melchitzedek Pinchas, guilty of this drek. My star will set. I'll be laughed at from the Hudson to the Jordan.

(struggling)

KLOOT

(impudently)

Hush, hush, you're interrupting the poesy.

PINCHAS

Who has drawn and quartered my play? Speak.

KLOOT

I've only arranged it for the stage.

PINCHAS

(flabbergasted)

You!

KLOOT

(with great assurance)

You said you and I are the only two men who understand how to treat poesy.

PINCHAS

You understand drek, not poesy. You conspire to keep me out of the theatre.... I will summons you.

KLOOT

(imperturbably)

We had to keep all the authors out. Suppose Shakespeare had complained of you?

PINCHAS

(modestly)

Shakespeare would have been only too grateful.

KLOOT

Hush, the boss is on.

POLONIUS

"He's coming. Now give it to him good."

QUEEN

"Will I ever?"

HAMLET

"Mother, mother, mother."

QUEEN

"Leave it to me."

POLONIUS

"I'll hide behind the curtain."

HAMLET

"Something wrong, Mom?"

QUEEN

"Hamlet, thou hast thy father much offended."

HAMLET

"Mother, you have my father much offended."

QUEEN

"Don't get fresh with your mother."

HAMLET

"Will you ever stop nagging?"

QUEEN

"Nagging. Now let me tell you...."

HAMLET

"I'm in no mood for fooling. You're going to listen."

QUEEN

"Let me go."

HAMLET

"Sit down. You shall not budge."

QUEEN

"Is this the way to treat your mother? I should die I have a son like this. Murder. Help. Help."

(Polonius stirs behind the curtain.)

HAMLET

"How, now, a rat?"

(Hamlet pulls his sword and runs Polonius through.)

POLONIUS

"Oy Veh!"

PINCHAS

(thunderstruck)

OY VEY!

(Pinchas makes a wild lunge, and is barely restrained by Kloot.)

KLOOT

Who's mutilating the poesy now? You'll spoil the scene.

PINCHAS

Liar, murderer. Word butcher. You promised me your wife as Ophelia.

KLOOT

Sure. The first wife I get, you shall have.

(Pinchas gnashes his teeth.)

KLOOT

I think you owe me a carfare.

PINCHAS

(icily)

Why is there singing in Hamlet?

KLOOT

Because it's Passover. You're a greenhorn. In New York it's a tradition to have musical plays on Passover. We only took your play as a Passover play.

PINCHAS

But Hamlet is not a musical play.

KLOOT

Yes it is. What about Ophelia's songs? That was what decided us. It only needed a little touching up by an experienced theatre person such as myself.

PINCHAS

But Hamlet is a tragedy!

KLOOT

Sure! They all die at the end. Our audiences are very compassionate. They'd be miserable if they didn't all die. Wait till they're dead, then you shall take your bow.

PINCHAS

Take my bow for your play!

KLOOT

There's quite a lot of your lines left, if you listen carefully. Only you're a poet and you don't understand stage technique. The idea was yours and was worth every cent we paid for it. Really, you're a genius.

(A storm of applause from the audience. The ghost cakewalks on stage and is confronted by Hamlet in mime.)

QUEEN

"I will not speak with her."

HORATIO

"Ophelia has gone meshugenah."

QUEEN

"Let her in."

OPHELIA

(tripping in)

I'm meshugenah,

Da, da, da,

I'm meshugenah,

Da, da, da,

Daddy's dead,

I'm out of my head....

(Ophelia's song is accompanied by incongruous music. The play continues in mime. Pinchas continues to struggle with Kloot.)

QUEEN

(to Hamlet)

"That Ophelia's a pain. I always told you you'd have trouble with shikses."

(The play continues in mime, to roars of approval.)

HAMLET

(with a skull)

"Oy Vey. Poor Yorick, I knew him well, Horatio. A real joker. An unemployed comedian...."

(Finally Pinchas escapes from Kloot and runs on stage brandishing his cane.)

PINCHAS

Cutter of lines.

(whacking Hamlet with his cane)

Perverter of poesy.

(whacking Hamlet again)

(The audience loves it; cheers as Hamlet runs off.)

PINCHAS

Good people. I am the world-famous poet, Melchitzedek Pinchas. This is not my play. This is not Shakespeare. This is drek! Drek!

(Kloot and other members of the cast drag off Pinchas.)

BLACKOUT

ACT V

The East Side Café, night.

It is later that night. Pinchas is sitting by himself in the deserted café. The bartender is polishing his glasses. Pinchas is sitting at a table.

Enter the Heathen Reporter.

REPORTER

Congratulations on your great success.

PINCHAS

(turning away)

Do not mock me!

REPORTER

But your Hamlet is a great hit. It's a sensation.

PINCHAS

It's a disgrace; a travesty! Poetry lies bleeding.

REPORTER

Well, you European intellectuals certainly take an odd view of things. I never laughed so hard in my life.

PINCHAS

You were not supposed to laugh. The play is a tragedy!

REPORTER

Maybe so, but I'd like to have a nickel for every ticket dollar that play will make.

PINCHAS

Bah! You're crazy. I'm going to stop them, no matter what. In the morning I will see Mendelsohn, the lawyer, and withdraw the right to produce my play.

(Enter Kloot.)

PINCHAS

You!

(rises and raises his cane)

Man of the Earth! Swindler! Enemy of Poetry!

KLOOT

Now you just hold on there, Pinchas—I've been looking for you all over the place.

PINCHAS

What do you want?

KLOOT

I came to give you your share of the box office.

PINCHAS

I don't want it.

KLOOT

The play's a hit. It will run for years. It's the greatest thing since sliced bread. You're a hero, Pinchas! You're famous.

PINCHAS

I'm a laughingstock. And because of you.

KLOOT

Now, that's what I want to talk to you about. You've got to do that thing again.

PINCHAS

What thing? What are you talking about?

KLOOT

You've got to run on stage and fight with everybody. Just like you did tonight. That was the showstopper.

PINCHAS

Are you mad?

KLOOT

Crazy like a fox, my boy. People almost pissed their pants.

PINCHAS

I will do no such thing!

KLOOT

That's O.K. we can have an actor playing you do it.

PINCHAS

I will not allow it! This whole travesty will stop tomorrow. I am going to Mendelsohn and he will put an end to this murder of art.

KLOOT

Say now, Pinchas, don't kill the goose that laid the golden egg.

PINCHAS

It will stop, I say.

KLOOT

Look here, Pinchas, here's $163.25—

PINCHAS

(turning)

I don't take bribes!

KLOOT

Bribes! Hain't no bribe. It's the author's share of the box office.

PINCHAS

For one night?

KLOOT

That's right. And, this play of yours, with a little help from yours truly, is likely to run a thousand and one nights as the saying goes.

PINCHAS

(musing)

A hundred and sixty-three dollars!

KLOOT

And twenty-five cents.

PINCHAS

It's more than I made in the last year.

KLOOT

And there's more where that come from. You are already being hailed as the comic genius from Warsaw.

PINCHAS

(unbelieving but flattered)

I am?

KLOOT

Damned right. What I want, what Goldwater wants, is another tragedy from you. He's ready to pay $200.00 in advance.

PINCHAS

Two hundred dollars!

(controlling himself)

No—I will not do it! I will not debase my art for any amount of money.

KLOOT

But....

REPORTER

But Mr. Pinchas, you're throwing away the opportunity of a lifetime. Not only will you get rich, but your fame, as the comic genius from Warsaw, will be jeopardized.

(Pinchas scowls. Putting his hands behind his back, he walks around in a circle considering—he waves his right hand muttering "On the one hand," then his left—"on the other hand," in considerable uncertainty. Finally, nodding to himself, he decides.)

PINCHAS

All right. But on one condition.

KLOOT

What's that?

PINCHAS

I will give you my Yiddish Caesar. I will let you butcher it to your heart's content. I will let you produce my Hamlet.

KLOOT

I'll treat it with the greatest respect. But what's your condition?

PINCHAS

My condition is that you don't try to stop me when I run on stage and beat Goldwater to death!

KLOOT

(thinking hard)

Well, you've got a deal.

(winking at the audience)

PINCHAS

Action is greater than thought.

KLOOT

(aside)

What do I care what happens to Goldwater?

CURTAIN

THE CONGRESSMAN'S NIGHTMARE

CAST OF CHARACTERS

Virgie Goodrich, a Congressional Aide, good-looking, but rather sexless in demeanor

Paul Horton, a distinguished, intellectual Congressman, in his mid-forties

Bill Walton, a Congressman of the poker-playing, hail-fellow-well-met variety, in his mid-forties

Man, a bill collector

Arlene, Horton's ex-wife, extremely attractive with an insinuating southern charm, in her mid-twenties

Vanessa Edmonds, a well-dressed, somewhat affected woman, in her late twenties

Diane Brennan, Vanessa's protégée and sidekick; a little younger than Vanessa, she tends to echo whatever Vanessa says

First and Second Sheiks, non-speaking roles[1]

---

1. The parts of the Sheiks may be doubled since they only appear in burnooses and robes at the end.

THE PLAY

The scene is Congressman Paul Horton's bachelor apartment. There is a piano and a couch. Several doors leading into the bedroom and other rooms in the apartment.

Virgie Goodrich is the Congressman's Aide and girl Friday (or as she would have it—"person Friday"). Virgie is all business, dressed in a unisex-style pantsuit with a string necktie. She is a model of aggressive dressing. Virgie is talking to a fairly well-dressed man who has come to collect a bill.

Virgie

I tell you, you cannot see the Congressman right now. He's in a conference and he won't be available for several hours.

Man (sitting down)

Then, I'll wait.

Virgie

Why don't you tell me what this is all about? I'm his Legislative Aide and I can probably handle it.

Man

It's not the sort of thing—

Virgie

You may wind up cooling your heels a long time if you don't.

Man

I'm sure the Congressman will prefer that I not discuss it with anyone but himself.

Virgie

You can leave your name and number with me. I'll have the Congressman call you.

Man

No.

Virgie

I don't like the tone of this. If you refuse to discuss the matter with me, I'll have to ask you to leave.

Man

The matter is personal.

Virgie

Either you explain it to me or you get out. If you don't get out, I'll have the police throw you out.

Man

You really put me in an awkward situation. Here! (giving her some papers) It's self-explanatory, and you can see why I thought it best to speak to the Congressman personally.

Virgie (gasping)

Oh, dear, this is too much.

Man

Will you pay it or not?

Virgie

This is more than I can manage. I'll speak to the Congressman.

(Enter Paul Horton from his study. Horton is a well-dressed, intellectual-looking man in his early forties.)

Paul

I'm Paul Horton. Can I help you? (to Virgie) I heard shouting. Is something wrong?

Virgie (giving Paul the papers)

Here, take a look. Two thousand dollars this time.

Paul

Whew! (to the Man) I am going to pay you. (the doorbell rings) Go get that, will you, Virgie?

(Exit Virgie.)

Man

I can wait.

Paul

Will you take a check?

Man

Certainly, Congressman.

Paul

I prefer to pay you in cash.

Man

I understand perfectly.

Paul

You'll have to wait a few minutes. I'm expecting some money shortly.

Man

I can be very patient.

(Enter Bill Walton, also a Congressman, accompanied by Virgie.)

Walton

It's me, old buddy.

Paul

Have you done what I asked you?

Walton

Certainly. (giving Paul a packet of money) Two thousand dollars. Sure you don't need more?

Paul

No, this is all. (counting it and giving it to the bill collector) Take it.

Man

Thank you very much. Here's your receipt. (gives a receipt) Sorry to trouble you, Congressman.

(Exit the Man, winking at Virgie, who gives him a frigid look.)

Paul

I'll repay you by the end of the month.

Walton

I'm not in any hurry.

Paul

It doesn't inconvenience you? At least—

Walton

Not at all. I won it at poker from our beloved President.

Paul

You're always lucky.

Walton

Good thing I am. Don't know how I'd manage on a Congressman's salary in this town if I weren't a good hand at poker.

Paul

The fact is—

Walton

Congressmen aren't paid enough.

Paul

Nobody makes enough. That's why misery is so widespread.

Virgie (seething and finally bursting out)

Do you know who this money is for, Mr. Walton?

Paul

Virgie, I wish you'd—uh—leave.

Virgie

I will not leave!

Paul

Then please shut up.

Virgie

I will not shut up!

Paul

I order you to shut up. There's no reason for you to tell Walton.

Virgie

You don't dare! (to Walton) Do you know for whom this money is?

Paul

Please, Virgie, please.

Walton

I really don't want to know. Paul asked me for a small loan, and what he does with the money, after all, is—

Virgie

Just so you'll know where your money's going. It's for the Congressman's wife—for his divorced, adulterous wife—who, since the divorce, has settled down to a comfortable and secure existence as a call girl.

Walton

For Arlene!

Virgie

Yes, sir, for Arlene! When she needs money—which is often—

who do you think she's cool enough to ask? It started two weeks after the divorce. One fine morning, Paul got a letter. (to Paul) Don't deny it, I've read it! (in a cloying tone) "Sweetie, I'm in an awful scrape. It would be so nice of you to send me five big ones." And he did it! After all she did to him. You understand, he's got a taste for this woman. Another time, it was a thousand, not five hundred. And I don't know how many other times. All to help her avoid some well-deserved disaster. And today, it's two thousand. (to Paul, who is still trying to shush her) You are not going to intimidate me! I am not going to let you ruin your career and simply hold my peace. When you got married, you were a successful lawyer with plenty of money in the bank, and a career that said you were headed for the Senate and maybe beyond. Now look at you! You've surrendered your fortune and you can't live off your salary as a Congressman. And why? Because you're a spendthrift? Hardly! For a creature who deceived you, who made you a laughingstock, and who totally disrupted your life! It's not just weakness, it's not just submitting to blackmail, it's—it's stupidity! And now that I have done my duty, I am going to get some work done.

(Virgie storms out with all flags flying.)

Paul

The only thing that prevents me from strangling her is that she is absolutely right.

Walton

Is it really true, Paul?

Paul

I'm afraid so.

Walton

You've been giving Arlene money?

Paul

What else can I do?

Walton

Just refuse and be firm about it. The divorce decree said no alimony and there were no children. You don't owe her a thing.

Paul

Legally, no.

Walton

Morally, you intend to say? After the life she led you before you divorced her? And if you had any obligation, any residual obligation, the life she's been leading since your divorce certainly discharges you of any obligation. She's practically, damn it, there's no blinking it: she's a prostitute.

Paul

Please don't say that.

Walton

Facts are facts, man. Or is she threatening you, blackmailing you?

Paul

No.

Walton

Is she saying that if you don't give her money, she'll let the world know she's your ex-wife, and a happy hooker to boot?

Paul

Arlene wouldn't do that. If there was even an implied threat, I wouldn't have anything to do with her.

Walton

Then, why'd you do it? If you had refused the first time, she would have sorted things out for herself, and wouldn't be bothering you anymore.

Paul

It was very difficult. She cried a lot.

Walton

She came here!

Paul

No—I begged her never to come here. She met me at the Smithsonian, and we—

Walton

She cried at the Smithsonian?

Paul

No, in my car.

Walton

Never mind. This is getting out of hand.

Paul

I am well aware.

Walton

You realize how close you are to being appointed Secretary of Defense? You realize what would happen if the President found out about this? Or the Press? Or Southwick? He wants to be Secretary of Defense so bad he'd feed his mother to the fish to get it. He'd think nothing of dragging your name in the mud.

Paul

I realize, I realize. Still, it's finished. I told Arlene this was the last time. That my position wouldn't permit me. She understood, and after that I didn't hear from her for about six months.

Walton

Still, she ought to be over her trouble. I saw her recently driving a Mercedes.

Paul

So much the better.

Walton

She gave me a friendly nod. I think she was with some Arab an ambassador or something.

Paul

That must be rough!

Walton

Let's hope. Because she's not really a bad kid.

Paul

No, not at all. She deceived me, without any treachery, naively, like a child that likes to rob the cookie jar. When I accused her, she admitted it and asked to be forgiven. So I forgave her. Then, the desire to play with the cookie jar came over her again. Just as nonchalantly as before.

Walton

It was a mistake to have married her.

Paul

I came to that conclusion. She's the kind of woman who should never marry. If she likes a man, she wants to go to bed with him. And she likes everybody.

Walton

I know it's hard to dislike her. How did she take the divorce?

Paul

As gaily as she took our marriage; she attaches no special importance to it. After the divorce she started working for an escort service, and in a short time she found her vocation.

Walton

And, neither of you bear each other any grudge?

Paul

Look, my God. I know what I'm doing is not very smart, or wise, or even moral as morality is understood, but what is there to say? Divorce ends the marriage but not the fact you've been married. When you've loved a woman, and lived with her for several years, it's naïve to think you'll be happy by getting rid of her. Whether you like it or not, you retain a certain feeling, just as you would for a pet, even though it bites you. And if it begs prettily, and wags its tail, you give it some sugar.

Walton

Well, ah, Arlene was certainly good at wagging her tail. Ha! Ha!

(There is the noise of a bell ringing.)

Walton

Couldn't help that one, Paul. Forgive me.

Paul

It wasn't an apt comparison, my own fault.

(Enter Virgie.)

Virgie (upset)

Paul—

Paul

What is it, Virgie?

Virgie

She is here!

Paul

Who's here?

Virgie

She. Your wife!

Walton

What, Arlene?

Virgie

Your wife! She's arguing with a cabby, but she's coming here.

Paul

Here? But she promised me. What's she going to do? What has she come for now?

Walton

She's come to beg for some sugar.

(Enter Arlene, a very good-looking woman dressed in the very latest fashion.)

Arlene (kissing Paul)

Darling! It's me. How are you, honey?

Paul (obviously glad to see her in spite of his apprehensions)

What a surprise!

Arlene

Yes, isn't it? (seeing Walton) What! Walton, I didn't see you. (hugging him, too) This is like old times.

Walton (somewhat stiffly, but not unfriendly)

Good to see you, Arlene.

Virgie (under her breath, but seething with venom)

She'd embrace the whole world, the little bitch.

Arlene

My little Virgie, you look great. I am going to get you a present.

Virgie

You're too good.

(Virgie goes out, frostily.)

Arlene

You can't imagine how happy I am to see you. I said to myself, perhaps he's still at his office.

Paul

I took leave.

Arlene

And you, too, Walton. I'm happy to see you again. I read in the papers that you've been reelected. That really pleases me.

Walton

Thanks, Arlene.

Paul

You need to talk to me, Arlene?

Arlene

I have so many things to tell you. (to Walton, who looks as if he's about to leave) But no, no, you're not in the way. You're a friend of the family.

Walton

But—

Paul (desperately)

Stay a while. I beg you. (insistently) I beg you, don't go.

Arlene (oblivious to the desperation in Paul's voice)

I've never been in your new apartment. Wow, you've bought a piano!

Paul

Fifty bucks a month.

Arlene

That's not expensive. It gives the place a touch of class. Ah, you've reupholstered the furniture. It really needed it. And then, you have a new clock. (laughing) Did you inherit some money?

Paul

No, no. On the contrary, I'm economizing.

Arlene

Well, your affairs are going better, and that's important. (taking his hands) I don't want you to be unhappy. That would make me very sad, you know, Paul.

Paul

I'm not unhappy. But I'm very concerned—

Arlene

Concerned about what?

Paul

Money. Ask Walton. He's the one who loaned me the money so I could pay your bill.

Arlene (puzzled)

What bill?

Paul (wondering how she could have forgotten)

The one I just paid for you. Two thousand dollars.

Arlene

Oh, now I remember.

Paul

The man came here to collect the money a little while ago. I paid him in cash.

Arlene

That was sweet of you. You did well. You always treat me right.

Paul

So now, I owe Walton two thousand dollars.

Arlene

Rest assured, my little Walton, he's going to pay you.

Walton (astounded by her audacity)

I don't doubt it for a minute.

Paul

But, you see the fix I'm in—

Arlene

Don't be afraid, darling. I didn't come for money.

Paul (prematurely relieved)

Ah, you didn't come for money?

Arlene

That would be taking advantage, and you know I never take advantage.

Paul

Oh, I can breathe again. That's nice. Isn't that nice, Walton?

Walton

Very nice.

Paul

You said just now that you had so many things—

Arlene

I'm getting to it. Kids, everything's in a mess for little old Arlene right now. You know I've been friends with Paul Hassan?

Walton

The Savaki Ambassador? No, I didn't know.

Arlene

He was the Savaki Ambassador until about a month ago. Now he's prime minister. We really had quite a thing going.

Paul

Very rich, I believe.

Arlene

Oh, you can't imagine. But, he has terrible taste, which I've tried to improve. Well anyway, we had quite a thing together until about six weeks ago. Then we had an unpleasant talk.

Paul

What was the little talk about?

Arlene

Stupid things. His Middle Eastern customs just are not civilized. I had supper with a few friends and he wasn't invited. He got angry and said some disagreeable things to me.

Paul

He got jealous.

Arlene

Oh, no. If I hadn't shown him the door, he would have walked out on me anyway. The man is absolutely medieval.

Paul

Go on.

Arlene

So when Hassan left, I found myself in a fix. He didn't leave me a penny. I pawned my jewels, but the money didn't last long.

Walton

What! Attractive as you are, you haven't latched on to someone new in six weeks?

Arlene (evasively)

Oh, I've had some dates. But no one serious has come along, and there are certain things I just cannot allow myself to do. In short, yesterday, after several reversals which wouldn't interest you, I had to sell off everything.

Paul

You sold your furniture?

Arlene

All, honey, except my bed.

Paul (taking her hand)

My poor Arlene.

Arlene

Oh, I don't repent it. I don't care about furniture and I've wanted to replace what I've had for some time.

Walton

You did the best thing.

Arlene

Only now, I have no place to live.

Paul

You haven't rented a place?

Arlene

Not yet. I've seen a very nice apartment for forty-one hundred a month in Georgetown—

Walton

Forty-one hundred a month?

Arlene

It's a steal at the price. How much do you pay here?

Paul (rather ashamed)

Eighteen hundred.

Arlene

Well, that's all right for a man, even a Congressman. You don't want the voters to think you live too well. But, for a woman, you understand— Anyway, I'm going to look around some more. I haven't decided.

Walton

That's wise.

Paul (naively)

And while waiting, you plan to stay with one of your girlfriends, I suppose?

Arlene

Oh, Vanessa Hughes offered me her apartment for several days, but I refused.

Paul

You should have accepted. You'd have been very happy with her.

Arlene (surprised)

You know Vanessa?

Paul

No, just an idea I had.

Arlene

It's perfectly conceivable you might. She goes everywhere. She's living with an undersecretary or something who's madly in love with her and is going to marry her, only he can't because he's already married and his wife won't divorce him.

Paul

Oh, I see. We'll have to wait for the wedding bells.

Arlene

She's charming, Vanessa, charming. But I don't want to owe her anything. I hate owing people anything. Then, I had another idea.

Paul (uneasily)

And that was?

Arlene

To stay with you for a while—until fortune turns my way again.

Paul (strangling)

With me?

Arlene

Naturally.

Paul

Here? You wish to take up residence here?

Arlene

Hell! You're my husband, after all, and nobody in the world can criticize us.

Paul

But, for God's sake, I am no longer your husband.

Arlene (innocently)

But, you were once—

Paul

I was once, that's true. But I am no longer. You understand that? We are DIVORCED officially!

Arlene

So what? What does that mean?

Paul

So what! You take my breath away. Ask Walton what that means.

Walton

The law is very clear.

Arlene

I don't give a damn about the law.

Walton (aghast)

Oh!

Arlene

So you won't have me?

Paul

I didn't say that! I tell you very gently that it's impossible for me. Quite impossible to hide you here.

Arlene

I have no idea of hiding.

Paul

This house is peaceful. I lead a regular life. I have my bachelor habits—most of them bad—and besides, I'm in line for a Cabinet position.

Walton (low to Paul)

Don't give her any ammunition.

Paul

If somebody heard a story like this, there'd be a scandal and I would be done for. You see how I trust you, I tell you everything.

Arlene

I wouldn't want to hurt your chances for anything, honey, but after our divorce you've been involved with women who aren't half as good as I am. So why?

Paul

I've never let any woman come here. Have I, Walton?

Walton

Not that I've heard of.

Arlene (bitterly disappointed, but not angry)

It's okay, honey, it's okay. I'm going.

(Arlene sits at the piano and plays the scales for a moment. Then she plays "La Vie en rose".)

Paul (to Walton)

Ah, great. That's all I needed. That was our song.

Walton

Be firm.

Paul

Do me justice, Arlene. Admit I've always been good to you. But this time I cannot. I swear to you, I cannot.

Arlene

You've always been wonderful to me, Paul. That's why I'll never forget you. I am not saying one word in reproach. You're acting perfectly within your rights. I will go to a hotel. I only want to stay here a short while to wait for my movers.

Paul

Movers?

Arlene

They're bringing my bed and clothes. I gave them your address. I was a little too sure of you. Don't worry, they won't come in. I'll tell Virgie to watch for them and I'll keep them from coming in.

Walton

My friend, I'm leaving. I have to meet with the President.

Paul

Speak to him about my business, will you?

(Arlene continues playing.)

Walton

That's why I came to see you.

Paul

And don't mention this.

Walton

Never fear.

Paul

I really should have had this appointment months ago.

Walton

I'm well aware of that.

Paul

Do you think I'll get the nomination?

Walton

I have reason to hope so.

Paul

It's my turn. I've earned it.

Walton

That's what's holding you back, you know. Bye, Arlene.

Arlene

Arrivederci, Walton.

Paul

You'll tell me the President's response?

Walton

As soon as I know it. He's cagey. (low) Don't weaken.

Paul

I am weak, that's true. But I am not an idiot.

Walton

Bye-bye, Arlene.

(Exit Walton.)

Arlene

Bye, honey.

(Arlene continues to play. After Walton leaves, Arlene suddenly stops playing and puts her head in her hand.)

Arlene

I haven't a chance, that's for sure.

Paul

But if— You're not reasonable and you don't manage your life properly.

Arlene (looking up)

You think so?

Paul

You need good advice.

Arlene

Give me some.

Paul

I've already given you plenty. I haven't got any more.

Arlene

You know, I've been looking forward to staying with you for several days, looking forward to taking a rest. I've been embarrassed, been kicked out, had all sorts of nasty things happen. It's no fun for a woman. I said to myself: "He's alone, he's a bachelor, he lives like a monk without any girlfriend. How would I bother him? And in the end, in spite of everything, he still cares for me. We remain friends." I guess I made a big mistake, that's all.

Paul

I've explained to you—

Arlene

That's all right. We won't speak about it anymore. (begins to cry)

Paul (to himself)

No, no. It would be too much of a blunder this time. (to Arlene) What's wrong?

Arlene

Nothing, really nothing.

Paul

Why do you cry?

Arlene

Don't pay any attention to it.

Paul

Look, don't put yourself in such a state. (wildly) You can stay a few days in a hotel, an agreeable hotel. I'll pay. My God, it won't kill you. If you need more money, I'll find some.

Arlene

Hotel rooms drive me to distraction. You know I've always been like that. I have to have beautiful things around me. I'll cry all day.

Paul

Aw, honey.

Arlene

Just four blank walls.

Paul

It just isn't possible for you to be here. And besides, if I let you stay, your little friends would be coming in and out at all hours—

Arlene

At first, no one will know I am here.

Paul

Oh.

Arlene

Except Vanessa, who is my best friend.

Paul

Already one too many.

Arlene

And then, I've told her not to come and see me unless she has something very important to tell me.

Paul

And she knows who I am?

Arlene

Oh, no! Vanessa is my intimate friend, but she really knows nothing about my life. I told her I was going to stay with a cousin. That's why I didn't give her the phone number. I have more tact and discretion than you think.

(putting her handkerchief to her eyes) I always look out for your interests.

Paul

Listen, Arlene, if you promise me, if you swear—

Arlene

I swear, darling.

Paul

If I was sure I wouldn't repent this—

Arlene

What must I swear?

Paul

I'll let you live here, and I'll give you some time—

Arlene

—For me to get things together. Oh, it won't be long. Oh, I'm so happy, my little sweetheart. How happy I am.

(kissing him)

Paul

It's absolutely agreed that this is only for a few days.

Arlene

But, of course. I never take advantage, as you know very well.

Paul

I am going to sleep on the couch. You stay in my room.

Arlene

But, I don't want to push you out of your own room, honey.

Paul (horrified)

Then—

Arlene (laughing)

Don't be stupid.

Paul (shocked)

Oh—

Arlene

What's so strange about that?

Paul

You don't seem to understand that what you are proposing is frightfully immoral?

Arlene

It's immoral?

Paul

Yes. Absolutely.

Arlene (childishly)

Why?

Paul

It would take too long to explain—and besides, I'm not sure that I know myself.

Arlene

All right. If you don't want to, I won't insist. I will sleep on the couch. But you know, I'm not an ingrate, and I don't take advantage. I just want to show you how much I appreciate all the sacrifices you make for me, and how much I still care for you.

Paul (uncomfortable)

No need to talk about all that.

Arlene

Yes, yes, there is. You are a nice guy. Do you know how few nice guys there are left in the world? When I think, you let me get the divorce—

Paul

For cruel and unusual treatment.

Arlene (laughing)

People would think you beat me. You might have trouble finding a new wife.

Paul (drily)

I'm in no hurry to remarry.

Arlene

Don't joke. You know there isn't one man in all the jet set I travel in that's half as nice as you.

Paul

Really?

Arlene

Honest Injun. And that's always been my opinion, always, even when I was stupid enough to cheat on you with that Senator. I didn't care for him half as much as I did for you.

Paul

No use recalling all that. What's past is past.

Arlene

It's all so sad when you think about it. I was so stupid. I thought I could have my cake and eat it too. I know better now. We were made for each other in so many ways. Unfortunately, I have a silly nature and never think about anything except the present. Why don't you marry again?

Paul

Oh, nobody wants me.

Arlene

Nonsense! Virgie would marry you in an instant.

Paul

Virgie?

Arlene

Don't you know she's crazy about you?

Paul

Why, for heaven's sake!

Arlene

You mean, you don't know, you big goof, that she's in love with you?

Paul

No. I guess not. She's very loyal. But I've never even thought of Virgie that way.

Arlene

Well, she's thought of you. I'm almost jealous and I would be if you liked her. Can't you see she's jealous of me?

Paul

Hmmm.

Arlene

Never mind Virgie. I will never forget how good you've been to me. (suddenly sitting on his lap) I hope someday you will get in some terrible trouble and I will be the only one who can save you. I won't hesitate, honey. I'll come right away.

Paul

What am I doing? Where am I heading?

Arlene

What's wrong?

Paul

Nothing.

Arlene (caressingly)

Nothing?

Paul

Get up. Please—get up.

(Enter Virgie, who stands and stares at first.)

Virgie

Sir.

Paul (helplessly)

What?

Virgie

There are two movers with some luggage and a—a bed.

Arlene

Ah. I'll take care of that.

(Arlene gets up and goes out.)

Virgie

Sir.

Paul

What? What?

Virgie

What should I do about the movers?

Paul

Whatever Arlene says.

Virgie (exploding)

Wonderful. (going out after Arlene) That's too much!

Paul

What a fool I am! What a fool! Wonderful. I'm in a pretty pickle. Let's see, let's see. Got to be calm. (practically dancing around) If this goes on much longer, I'll marry her again. I can't send her away now. I can't do it. I've got to find another way.

(Reenter Virgie.)

Virgie (holding out her hand)

Some money, please.

Paul

Why?

Virgie (icily)

For the movers.

Paul (giving her some money)

Here.

Virgie

What shall I tell the building manager?

Paul

Nothing, you understand? Nothing!

Virgie

Excuse me, Congressman. I must have some explanation about your wife. The manager believes that you are a bachelor, and everybody has seen a woman enter here. With a lot of luggage. It's already on its way to being a scandal. Several neighbors are watching from their windows. What do I say? What answer to I give?

Paul

Tell them whatever you like. I really don't care.

Virgie

Oh. In that case, I don't either. I will say that you are divorced, but that you are reconciling with your wife who just happens to be a call girl.

Paul

Virgie, I know you are furious with me, but please, don't make things more difficult than they are. Say—never mind what—say she's my cousin or my niece. Flew in from the coast.

Virgie

Who's just graduated from college.

Paul

That's the stuff.

Virgie

And has come to D.C. for a visit.

Paul

Exactly.

Virgie

They'll never believe it.

(Enter Arlene.)

Arlene

Virgie, they're waiting for you. Ah, Paul, I forgot. Can you give me a twenty?

Paul

Why not? In for a nickel, in for a dime.

Arlene

To buy some flowers. Hurry up. (Paul gives her the money and she gives it to Virgie) Virgie, would you go to a florist and buy us some flowers?

Virgie (incensed)

Twenty dollars' worth of flowers!

Arlene

Hurry up. And pay the movers on your way out, will you?

Paul

Go ahead.

(Virgie leaves, vowing who knows what kind of unspeakable vengeance on Arlene.)

Arlene

Really, your place is a little sad.

Paul

I never noticed.

Arlene

Leave it to me to liven it up. You've got a couple of horrid vases by the chimney, but with flowers they won't be too bad. Men. Take the piano, for instance. It ought to be in the corner. You just don't know how to decorate.

Paul

Move it if you like. (to himself) It's starting again. It's happening all over again. She's taking over. (to Arlene) And the sofa? You haven't said anything about the sofa.

Arlene

The sofa. No, it's not right either. I think I'll put it over there. (pointing)

Paul

There! That's where the piano should be. And the piano is in the place of the table. And the table in place of the armchair. Let's change everything, everything!

Arlene

Oh yes, oh yes. Let's have some fun.

Paul

Put everything topsy-turvy. Upset everything. Go on, don't hesitate. You are in your role and I have no objections. Do what you have to do!

(There is a noise of someone entering. Enter Vanessa Edmonds and Diane Brennan, both very good-looking and fashionably dressed.)

Vanessa (hugging Arlene)

Ah, my dear. What a funny little apartment. The doorman tried to stop us from coming in.

Diane

Yes, dear, he tried to stop us.

Arlene

What a surprise! You both look real nice.

Paul (to himself)

Now what's going to happen?

Arlene

In fact—(to Paul) Let me present Miss Vanessa Edmonds and Miss Diane Brennan, two good friends of mine.

Vanessa (in stilted French)

Enchanté, Monsieur.

Diane

Delighted. Arlene has spoken to us about you.

Paul (strangled)

Has she? How nice of her.

Vanessa

Often. We are close friends of your niece. We have no secrets from one another.

Paul

Then you must have a lot to discuss. I ask your permission, ladies—

Vanessa

Goodbye, sir. Au revoir. Very happy to have made your acquaintance.

Paul (leaving, muttering to himself)

Forward, march. Make a decision or all is lost forever.

Vanessa

Your uncle looks familiar.

Arlene

Really?

Diane

One of your clients, perhaps?

(Arlene looks vexed.)

Vanessa

Oh, no. I never forget a client. No. He looks so distinguished. I think I've seen him or someone who looks like him on TV.

Arlene

Oh, everybody thinks they've seen uncle Paul somewhere.

Diane

He looks like a Congressman or Senator, that's what he looks like.

Arlene

Paul will be flattered.

Diane

I mean it.

Vanessa

Your uncle is kind of cute, honey, but that's not why we came.

Diane

We have some good news to bring you.

Arlene

Well?

Vanessa

We know a man who is crazy in love with you. I mean crazy in love!

Diane

Yes, honey. Crazy in love.

Arlene

Really. Who is he?

Vanessa

A very wealthy john.

Diane

A sheik.

Arlene

A sheik?

Vanessa

A sheik who is immensely wealthy, and who owns ever so many oil wells.

Arlene

I've had enough of sheiks.

Vanessa

Not this one.

Diane

Kehadi.

Arlene

I seem to recall.

Vanessa

You ought to recall. I introduced him to you once.

Arlene

A little bit fat. Sleek like a greased pig?

Diane

He's charming.

Vanessa

He just may be the richest man in the world.

Arlene

And you say he's in love with me?

Diane

Exactly, darling.

Arlene

Why didn't he tell me himself?

Vanessa

He didn't dare. He's very timid and besides, you were balling Hassan at the time. So he went back to his home or somewhere to pine for you.

Arlene

To his harem, I bet.

Diane

But in despair.

Arlene

And now he's back?

Vanessa

As soon as he heard you and Hassan had broken up, he came on his personal jet. He flew in yesterday, tried to find you, but couldn't, and came to me to find out what had become of you. In my place some other woman would have told him that Hassan had kicked you out and tried to take over this new little sheik for herself. But not me. I am a good friend.

Diane

And me, too.

Arlene

I thank you both.

Vanessa

You'd really have to see what a state he was in, the poor dear man. After I told him everything, he radiated, my dear, he simply radiated. There isn't any other word for it. "Then she's free," he cried. He had such an ecstatic expression on his face, dear, like he died and went to heaven. A real chump. But we shouldn't speak evil of chumps. Without them, how could we live so well in this city?

Arlene

And so—

Vanessa

And so, he thinks only of you. He begged me to tell him where you were living.

Arlene (uneasy)

I hope you didn't tell him.

Vanessa

Not at first, because you told me to be discreet. But he went wild, actually started crying real tears in his voice. In the end, I did because I was sure I was doing you a good turn. He's giving me a Jaguar, by the way, to thank me. He'll be here any minute.

Arlene

Here?

Vanessa

Of course here.

Arlene

I really can't receive him. I'm not in my own apartment.

Vanessa

The sheik is a man who is very well brought up.

Diane

He can be presented anywhere.

Vanessa

Why, he goes to the White House.

Diane

In short, you've got to—

Vanessa

If you don't, I may not get my Jaguar—

Diane

He can be presented to your uncle, and more than once!

Arlene

But my uncle is not my uncle!

Vanessa

Oh!

Diane

That's the trouble?

Arlene

That's the trouble.

Vanessa

But he's a man you can wrap around your little finger. He's young, he's rich, he's naïve, and he's fired up. For you. A naïve, rich man who's willing to do anything for you. It's a dream come true. I've never been able to find a john like that. When I do—

Diane

Me either.

Vanessa

Believe me, don't discourage him. I'm advising you as a friend.

(A noise is heard in the hallway.)

Diane

Maybe that's him now.

(Enter Walton, visibly surprised to see the three women together.)

Walton

Oh! Excuse me.

Arlene

Hello again, my dear little Walton.

Walton

I've got to speak to Paul. Is he still here?

Arlene

Of course, of course. Congressman Walton, two good friends of mine.

Vanessa

Oh, I know this gentleman. I saw him the other day in the House.

Walton

What day, Miss?

Vanessa

The day you were speaking on taxes. You were really giving it to the opposition. Who was that man you were insulting?

Walton

I have forgotten. Probably a good friend.

Diane

You were really great.

Walton

Were you there, too, Miss?

Diane

I sure was.

Walton

I wouldn't think a debate on taxes would interest such lovely ladies.

Vanessa

Oh, we weren't there for the debate. We were showing some friends around town, and they wanted to see the Congress in action.

Diane

Goodbye, Mr. Walton.

Walton

Goodbye, Miss.

Vanessa (seductively)

Till we meet again, Mr. Walton.

Walton (troubled)

Till we meet again, Miss.

(Arlene takes her friends out. After a minute, Paul enters.)

Walton

What is going on here?

Paul

Ah, I need you, good buddy.

Walton

What?

Paul

I've done it. I really have done it this time.

Walton

You've done something stupid?

Paul

Arlene cried. And I felt something. I had this stupid feeling, this stupid emotion of compassion. I'm letting her stay. Don't chastise me for it. The mistake is made. The question is how to straighten things out. Walton, think of something.

Walton

I really don't know. And I have to leave immediately.

Paul

You are leaving? You are abandoning me? Where are you going?

Walton

The President asked me to undertake a confidential mission for him.

Paul

Walton, I am going to find out if you are a true friend—

Walton

You doubt it?

Paul

Take me along.

Walton

I couldn't ask for anyone better.

Paul

Take me. It's the only way. As long as I stay in Washington, I'll never free myself of her, I know it.

Walton

You're right.

Paul

I will leave Arlene with Virgie. I don't care so long as I am not here.

Walton

I have to stop at my house to pack.

Paul

That will give me time to pack, too.

(Enter Arlene.)

Paul

Arlene.

Arlene

Honey.

Paul

Walton has just brought me some news that makes it necessary for me to leave Washington for several weeks. I have to go immediately.

Arlene (taking his hands)

Not bad news, I hope?

Paul

No, on the contrary. Good.

Arlene

That's good, honey. You had me worried for a minute. Where are you going?

Paul

Where are we going, Walton?

Walton

Oh, it's a secret. We're on a special mission.

Arlene

Hey, that's great. When will you be coming back?

Paul

I can't say. You can stay here as long as you like. I'll give Virgie some money for you, which Walton will loan me.

Walton

Right, right—

Paul

I only ask that you don't break anything.

Arlene

I promise.

Paul

And no wild parties, okay?

Arlene

What kind of girl do you think I am, anyway? Really, I don't think I'll be here very long. There's this gentleman who—

Paul

Hell! You shouldn't mention a thing like that to me. When you go, simply notify Virgie. She'll let me know.

Arlene

Do you want me to call or write?

Paul

No use. I don't know where I'll be.

Walton (looking at his watch)

We've got to hurry.

Paul

Give me five minutes. (calling) Virgie!

(Enter Virgie.)

Virgie (frigidly)

Yes, Congressman.

Paul

Virgie, be a dear, pack my suitcase.

Virgie (astounded)

You're leaving?

Paul

Yes, I'm leaving with Congressman Walton on a hush-hush trip. Go on, hurry up. Pack my suitcase, everything for a long trip.

Virgie (going out)

I am going, sir, I am going.

Paul

Walton, will you lend me—

Walton (pulling out a check and signing it)

Here, it's blank. Use it as you like.

Paul (giving it to Arlene)

Here, baby— (writing in a sum)

Arlene (kissing Paul)

Thanks, darling, thanks.

Paul

Do you have enough?

Arlene

This will be plenty. And I am going to economize.

Paul

Yes, be prudent. With your carefree disposition, all you need is a little prudence to lead a happy life.

Arlene

My God! I've done so many stupid things.

Paul

True. But you had legitimate excuses. You have even more excuses than you know. Now Arlene, we are going to separate, and it is very likely we won't see each other for quite a long time.

Arlene

That will break my heart, you know, darling.

Paul

Mine also. But what do you want? You have your interests, and I have mine. They are too different for us to see each other often. Think of the future, my poor little Arlene. You won't always be young and pretty. Make hay while the sun shines.

Arlene

Where am I going to find another guy like you? If I do, I'm going to marry him.

(Virgie returns, carrying a suitcase and a briefcase.)

Paul

Everything's ready?

Virgie

Would you please check to see?

Paul

No, no. You always do it right, Virgie. It's fine, I know. Virgie—while I'm gone, you look after Arlene.

Virgie (totally confused)

What? She's not going with you?

Paul

No remarks, please. Yes, my wife is staying here. And I want you to obey her and look out for her. I'll write or call soon.

Arlene

Don't make such big eyes, Virgie.

Virgie (stalking out in a fury)

As the Congressman likes.

Walton

Have you got everything you need? Let's go.

Arlene

Here, Walton, before you go, I want to ask—

Walton

Ask what, Arlene?

Arlene

Did you see the President?

Walton

Yes, I just got back.

Arlene

Well? What did he say about Paul?

Walton

He said Paul is the most qualified candidate.

Arlene

Wow! Congratulations, honey.

Walton

Not so fast. There are other considerations besides ability.

Arlene

He'd better appoint Paul, or I am going to have some words with him.

Walton

He's cagey, is our President. He hasn't made up his mind yet. Wouldn't tell even me.

Arlene

Paul's going to get it. I know. I have this feeling.

Paul

Anyway, I've got to go. Let's see. My hat. An umbrella, just in case. (noises at the door) Now, who can that be?

Arlene

It's probably a visitor for me.

(Enter Virgie.)

Virgie

Two gentlemen to see the lady. For you, Arlene.

Paul

You see, it's best that I go. We'll go down the back stairs. (hugging Arlene) Goodbye, baby. (grabs his suitcase and briefcase)

Arlene

Goodbye, my darling, goodbye, Walton.

Paul

Au revoir, Virgie. I'll write soon. (to Walton) This time I'm going to save myself.

(Exit Paul and Walton hurriedly.)

Virgie

And those gentlemen?

Arlene

Tell them to come in. I'm going to freshen up first.

(Exit Arlene.)

Virgie (sniffing)

Today, two. Tomorrow it will be four. (the phone rings, Virgie answers) Congressman Horton's. What? No, the Congressman has no statement to make about that rumor. What do you mean it's not a rumor? The appointment is on its way to the Senate? (the phone rings) Just a moment, sir. I have to get the other line. (putting the present caller on hold) Congressman Horton's, can you hold? What? What? Yes, Mr. President, I'll try to get him.

(screaming) Paul, Paul, you stupid son-of-a-bitch, you've just been appointed Secretary of Defense!

(Virgie runs to the door yelling. As she turns around she sees two men have entered. They are dressed in white robes with

Arabic burnooses. They look puzzled. When Virgie sees them, she screams loud and long. Arlene enters with her make-up only partly on.)

Arlene

Virgie, have you gone mad?

Virgie

Paul is Secretary of Defense, Paul is Secretary of Defense!

Arlene

Well, that's great. I told you I knew he was going to get it. Trust my feelings. (to the Arabs) Excuse me, gentlemen. Be right back.

(Arlene goes out unconcernedly as the curtain falls. Virgie continues to scream. The Arabs salaam.)

CURTAIN

THE MOONSHINE VINE

CAST OF CHARACTERS

The Lady

Her PAUL

The Washerwoman

The Old Woman

The Police Officer

A Marine

A Cow

A Butcher

5 men, 3 women with the possibility of doubling some parts.

The Moonshine Vine is an adaptation of an anonymous French play, of the type that used to be staged at fairs in the nineteenth century. It's been given an American setting.

THE PLAY

The action takes place in a rural area of a an unidentified country.

The stage represents a comfortable room. A person is seated at a table covered with manuscripts. He's working seriously, which is proved by the fact he consults a large dictionary from time to time. His wife, who is young and pretty, rushes in, very fashionably dressed.

WIFE:

I'm ready! (Paul turns the pages of the dictionary with close attention) (louder) I am ready!

PAUL:

(still at his dictionary) So much the better!

WIFE:

Look at me!

PAUL:

(nose in his dictionary) I am looking at you.

WIFE:

Liar!

PAUL:

(still working) Me? A liar?

WIFE:

You told me you are looking at me, and you're not looking at me. You're looking at your old book.

PAUL:

(still fumbling through his dictionary) Excuse me, my work—

WIFE:

(weeping) You don't love me anymore!

PAUL:

(raising his head) Yes, yes, I do. But my work.

WIFE:

(squeaking like a rabbit) Am I not well dressed, well made up, and well shod? (showing him her legs)

PAUL:

(staring flabbergasted) Oh!

WIFE:

I am very pretty. I know it! My mirror told me so.

PAUL:

Huh?

WIFE:

(letting her skirt fall) Tell me the same thing as my mirror.

PAUL:

Eh!

WIFE:

Have you finished bleating?

PAUL:

But—

WIFE:

Don't you realize that you are bleating?

PAUL:

No.

WIFE:

Then—you're dumb.

PAUL:

Oh!

WIFE:

All you say is oh, ah, eh, but, huh. (tearfully) I am not happy.

PAUL:

Why aren't you happy? I leave you alone.

WIFE:

That's what displeases me! Occupy yourself with me instead of sticking your nose in your scribblings all the time.

PAUL:

(eyes to heaven) To call the most scientific research scribblings!

WIFE:

By the way. What are you working on?

PAUL:

(gravely) The origins of the universe.

WIFE:

That's something that took place a long while ago.

PAUL:

That's why it's so difficult.

WIFE:

How sad it is to have a Paul who concerns himself with antiquarian things instead of admiring his wife in detail. (pulling up her skirt) Why, look at my legs.

PAUL:

Yes, yes, Very fine quality.

WIFE:

(letting her skirt fall) That's not what you should have said.

PAUL:

(in despair, hands over his face) My head! My poor head!

WIFE:

You should have said: oh, what beautiful legs.

PAUL:

(calmly) What beautiful legs.

WIFE:

You say it mechanically.

PAUL:

(sighing) I say it as I think it.

WIFE:

Say it with more enthusiasm.

PAUL:

(calmly) What pretty legs.

WIFE:

That's still mechanical.

PAUL:

(exhausted) You wear me out.

WIFE:

That's just the way men are! Love for them is just a brush fire. Soon out. Only women know how to love.

PAUL:

But—

WIFE:

And who remain attached to the object of their desire.— Come with me.

PAUL:

Where are you going?

WIFE:

To my cousin's. She doesn't live far away. A short walk.

PAUL:

Impossible! My work.

WIFE:

You've always disliked my family. You don't want to come to her party. It's her birthday. You prefer to busy yourself with idiocies, your origins of the universe!

PAUL:

Excuse me! They are not idiocies. There is nothing more serious than the origins of the universe.

WIFE:

Well, stay with them! I'm in my killing clothes. There will be men at my cousin's. Men who will know how to appreciate the beauty of my gorgeous legs.

PAUL:

(starting) All the same! You aren't going to show your legs to your cousin's guests.

WIFE:

(scornfully) Don't worry. I know how to behave in society. I'll find a good pretext.

PAUL:

That's preposterous.

WIFE:

What is preposterous is a Paul who abandons his wife, who is dressed up to annihilate other women at her cousin's party with her elegance.

PAUL:

If you want to annihilate the other ladies at your cousin's party with your elegance, you don't need any help from me. I have no thought of annihilating them.

WIFE:

Oh! Paul! Paul! Paul!

PAUL:

I know my name is Paul.

WIFE:

You will live to regret your attitude. Goodbye! Remain with the origins of the universe! As for me, I am going to deploy my charms in an assembly of the highest society. Goodbye, Paul. May you not regret your indifference to the feelings of an ardent and passionate wife. (she leaves abruptly)

PAUL:

(fists at his temple) Ouf! Ouf! Where was I? In the year 16,294 before Prince Mini of Egypt, who lived 5,000 years before our era— My head, my poor head. (someone knocks)

(A very pretty girl enters.)

WASHERWOMAN:

Sir—the washerwoman.

PAUL:

(nose in his dictionary) Put the linen in the kitchen.

WASHERWOMAN:

Sir, I didn't bring any!

PAUL:

(nose still in his dictionary) Oh, you've come for the dirty linen? I don't know where it is. My wife went out.

WASHERWOMAN:

How lucky.

PAUL:

To whom are you speaking?

WASHERWOMAN:

That woman is always in the way.

PAUL:

I'm at the point of proving that steam was first utilized in the year 70,294 before Mini—

WASHERWOMAN:

Sir, I love you.

PAUL:

(startled) Huh? What did you say?

WASHERWOMAN:

(speaking in a monotonous tone) Sir, it's been a long while since I wrote a letter on this paper. I am going to read it to you and I've learned it by heart. "Sir, I love you. You are my only thought, my only ideal, and my only happiness. Sir! I think about you day and night; in the day my thoughts fly towards you, and at night I imagine you are stretched out in my bed, which is a proof of love no one can dispute. I love you. In my eyes you are an accomplished man, handsome, distinguished, intelligent. All other men seem to me, in comparison to you, stupid, inept, insipid. I love you, I suffer that you are married, for I was the woman God intended for your wife. I know that you are united by sacred chains, but I can no longer submit to my martyrdom. I love you. I must tell you of my love. It's too strong for me. I know that, acting as I am, I am committing a great sin, but I am going to confess myself. I love you. You are my idol. And that's all."

PAUL:

Get hold of yourself, miss.

WASHERWOMAN:

I waited for the departure of your spouse to come make my

declaration.

PAUL:

I'm very much obliged to you for it.

WASHERWOMAN:

Tell me that you love me.

PAUL:

Listen, miss, you surprise me in the midst of my work.

WASHERWOMAN:

You are a very intelligent man, right?

PAUL:

Oh!

WASHERWOMAN:

You must understand this is a great love.

PAUL:

You take me a little unawares.

WASHERWOMAN:

Don't you find me pretty?

PAUL:

(looking at her) Yes, indeed, yes, indeed.

WASHERWOMAN:

(pulling up her skirt) Look at the pretty stockings I put on for you!

PAUL:

Evidently. They're very pretty.

WASHERWOMAN:

You say nothing of the legs in those stockings.

PAUL:

I mean ah!

WASHERWOMAN:

I'll show you that, too. This is only the beginning.

PAUL:

You are goodness itself, miss, and believe me, I am very sensible of—

WASHERWOMAN:

(letting her skirt fall) Kiss me, if you please.

PAUL:

Frankly, miss, you make me rather very uncomfortable.

WASHERWOMAN:

Oh. No need to be uncomfortable with me!

PAUL:

My wife isn't here.

WASHERWOMAN:

That works out fine. When you kiss a woman not your wife, surely it's when your wife is not around.

PAUL:

And she might return at any minute.

WASHERWOMAN:

Where did she go?

PAUL:

To her cousin's on the other side of a little woods.

WASHERWOMAN:

On the other side of a little woods? You'll never see her again.

PAUL:

Don't give me hopes.

WASHERWOMAN:

You don't believe me! Are you unaware that in the little woods there is a vine called the Moonshine Vine? It causes those who tread on it to lose their way and gives them the most bizarre looks.

PAUL:

Miss, I am a scientist to whom one must not tell old wives' tales.

WASHERWOMAN:

Sir, I am not an old wife! (weeping) Oh, you treat me like an old wife. That's not nice! All the same— (pulling up her skirts) Look at my legs! Don't they please you?

PAUL:

I told you before already. They please me a lot.

WASHERWOMAN:

I love you!

PAUL:

I am very grateful to you for it.

WASHERWOMAN:

(letting her skirt fall) Well, then kiss me.

PAUL:

My work prevents me.

WASHERWOMAN:

Don't hold yourself back!

PAUL:

I am a man of learning.

WASHERWOMAN:

Well, study me.

PAUL:

I am overwhelmed, miss.

WASHERWOMAN:

That's not enough! I love you. Tell me you love me!

PAUL:

The world took hundreds of millions of years to form—

WASHERWOMAN:

Love is quicker. Do I please you? Or don't I please you?

PAUL:

You are very pretty, that's evident.

WASHERWOMAN:

Then what are you waiting for? Embrace me! What? In despair, I, too, will go into the little wood where the Moonshine Vine will cause me to vanish to I-don't-know-where and change me into I-don't-know-what!

PAUL:

After all, you're right! You are charming and desirable! Ah? My wife treats me like a pen pusher and a library rat. Wait a bit!

WASHERWOMAN:

I am waiting. But waiting is tiresome.

PAUL:

After all, I'm a man like other men. An opportunity presents itself. Go to it! (jumps on her)

WASHERWOMAN:

Ah—Paul!

PAUL:

You know my name?

WASHERWOMAN:

Yes, my Paul. Ah, how nice it is in your arms.

PAUL:

Is it true?

WASHERWOMAN:

Is it ever true? Happily your wife will never return, thanks to the Moonshine Vine.

PAUL:

Let's hope so! What's your name?

WASHERWOMAN:

My name is Pauline.

(The door opens and a filthy old woman appears. A kind of ragged sorceress with a wand.)

OLD WOMAN:

This is nice!

PAUL:

Indeed, I think it is nice. She's a washerwoman.

OLD WOMAN:

The situation is dramatic! A Paul has a woman not his wife clasped in his arms. The man is ridiculous to the whole world.

PAUL:

I ask myself, what's it to you if I kiss a woman not my wife?

WASHERWOMAN:

She's unbalanced.

OLD WOMAN:

Miserable accomplice of an unworthy Paul, I will not allow you to insult a woman who is distinguished, elegant, and ravishing. Vanish, girl from nowhere. Cajoler of men who belong to others. Or I'll break my stick on your back.

WASHERWOMAN:

Put yourself in front of me, my dear love, so that the blows from her stick will fall on you and not on me.

PAUL:

(pursued by the old woman and shielding the washerwoman with his body from her blows) Old sorceress, I order you to get out of here!

OLD WOMAN:

(brandishing her stick) Not satisfied with surrendering yourself to lust with someone other than me, you intend for me to sacrifice myself to your filthy work.

PAUL:

I forbid you to speak to me like that!

OLD WOMAN:

(stopping, eyes to heaven) A fine creature! To make me get out of my own home!

PAUL:

You don't understand what that means in plain English?

OLD WOMAN:

Plain English? You've got some nerve!

WASHERWOMAN:

She stepped on the Moonshine Vine. She doesn't realize what she's become.

PAUL:

Stop flourishing that big stick. You are going to do some harm.

OLD WOMAN:

You take my umbrella for a big stick. You are hallucinating.

PAUL:

Pauline, go find a cop to arrest this intruder.

OLD WOMAN:

Intruder? In my own home? I'm going to beat you unmercifully.

PAUL:

Hurry, Pauline!

(Pauline rushes out. The Old Woman drops her stick.)

OLD WOMAN:

Now that she's gone, I am ready to forgive you!

PAUL:

Forgive me for what?

OLD WOMAN:

Don't be an imbecile! Your only excuse is that you are behaving like all other men when the opportunity presents itself.

PAUL:

(picking up the stick and holding it firmly with both hands behind his back) My good woman—

OLD WOMAN:

I forbid you to call me your good woman! I am in the Spring of my youth.

PAUL:

I have had enough of this. The young girl—

OLD WOMAN:

(dramatically) That you were kissing!

PAUL:

That young woman was recounting a tale of the Moonshine Vine which doesn't grow on the brain of my skeptical science.

OLD WOMAN:

You are right. She babbles stupidities! Fall in my arms! All is forgiven. With men, women have to be flexible.

PAUL:

Decamp immediately!

OLD WOMAN:

At the moment I am showing you great indulgence, I beg you: don't be vulgar!

PAUL:

If you don't decamp—

OLD WOMAN:

Again?

PAUL:

The cop will throw you in jail.

OLD WOMAN:

In jail? Me?

PAUL:

Listen! Let's stop this. What is it you want? Charity? You have a funny way of asking for it—!

OLD WOMAN:

Yes, it's charity I ask for! The charity of your inviolate love despite your culpable weakness for the washerwoman. My poor friend, I see how things stand. You stepped on the Moonshine Vine and your wits are turned. You don't recognize me.

PAUL:

The Moonshine Vine again! You are getting on my nerves.

OLD WOMAN:

Paul, Paul. Remember me. (she pulls up her skirts) Look at my legs. They are the most beautiful in the country.

PAUL:

Leave the country in peace.

OLD WOMAN:

Paul— You are hurting me a lot.

PAUL:

Lower your skirt. It's indecent.

OLD WOMAN:

Beauty is never indecent.

PAUL:

You are suffering from delusions! I order you to stop this disturbing exhibition and lower your skirt.

OLD WOMAN:

(letting her skirt fall) So be it! But tell yourself your stupidity excuses your fault. You no longer know what you are doing or you wouldn't have kissed the washerwoman. I am going to bring you back to me, to care for you! To pet you! To cover you with kisses.

PAUL:

And the cop doesn't come!

OLD WOMAN:

(jumping on him) Ah! I've got you! Paul! Remember our embrace! I will save you from your dreadful illness.

PAUL:

Will you kindly release me?

OLD WOMAN:

Smell my hair!

PAUL:

Smell your scrubby wig! How horrible!

OLD WOMAN:

I will never let you go again.

PAUL:

Have you finished choking me?

(The Washerwoman returns.)

WASHERWOMAN:

The cop is not at his post. (pathetically) Oh, Paul. What you are doing is criminal. To cheat on a love like mine with an old monster. After I've destroyed myself, you'll be remorseful. But it will be too late!

OLD WOMAN:

Don't listen to her. She has surely trampled on the Moonshine Vine and she, too, cannot see my beauty.

WASHERWOMAN:

I who am young and in the Spring of my youth. Must I see the man I love in the arms of an octogenarian!

OLD WOMAN:

The Spring of my youth is worth more than yours, my little one.

PAUL:

This situation cannot continue!

OLD WOMAN:

That's my opinion, indeed.

(Pauline curls up in the chair and peeks into the scribblings.)

PAUL:

(desperately trying to free himself from the grasp of the old woman) Pauline, I beg you, don't soak my documents on the origin of the universe with your tears! That's going to screw everything up!

PAULINE:

(tearfully) You don't love me anymore.

PAUL:

(still trying to free himself) For once I was at peace without my wife and I could follow my inclinations. Here comes this old vampire who ruins a unique opportunity.

OLD WOMAN:

Paul! You're going beyond all bounds!

PAULINE:

(in tears) You can't expect anyone to believe that you can't break the grip of an octogenarian! You must be a pervert! Ah, my life is ruined!

PAUL:

Ah? I can't break the grip, eh? That's too much. Pauline, you are going to see what you are going to see! (dragging the old woman to the door)

OLD WOMAN:

Paul! Don't jostle me.

PAUL:

From respect for your sex, I've kept within polite bounds. But I no longer know them. (pulling her violently towards the door)

OLD WOMAN:

(clinging to him) Paul! What you are doing exceeds in horror the greatest infamies committed since the creation of the universe!

PAUL:

The creation of the universe is my business! (he hurls her out the door)

OLD WOMAN:

(shouting outside) Paul! Paul! I am going to show my legs to all my cousin's guests. That's what you are asking for!

PAUL:

(going to Pauline, hiccupping) What a scandal! What an unbelievable scandal! Look, Pauline, you don't for a minute think being hugged by a witch gives me any pleasure, do you?

PAULINE:

She's not a witch—she's your wife.

PAUL:

I beg you not to keep saying that!

PAULINE:

It's the truth! And I was crying because you were in your wife's arms!

PAUL:

Be reasonable, Pauline. Come on, kiss me.

PAULINE:

I forgive you, but—you don't deserve it.

PAUL:

Come to my arms! (they entwine and kiss)

PAULINE:

I am feeling better!

PAUL:

So much the better

PAULINE:

Kiss me some more. (they kiss again)

PAUL:

What a contrast with the other one.

PAULINE:

There's nothing special about me?

PAUL:

She wanted me to smell her hair!

PAULINE:

Smell mine!

PAUL:

As you wish!

PAULINE:

(pulling away with a distracted air) Ah! Ah! Ah!

PAUL:

What's wrong with you?

PAULINE:

After she stepped on the Moonshine Vine she was changed into an octogenarian. If only that were forever. If she steps on it again, she's capable of becoming as beautiful as she was before. (tearfully) I will never be reconciled to that!

PAUL:

Ravishing Pauline, once and for all, forget that ridiculous superstition; it is unworthy of the century in which we live.

PAULINE:

You are right to say you are a skeptic.

PAUL:

Stop this unreasonable nonsense.

PAULINE:

When a woman is in love, she's always uneasy.

PAUL:

Pauline, throw yourself into my arms.

PAULINE:

(in his arms) With pleasure.

PAUL:

Kiss me.

PAULINE:

(kissing him) Effusively!

PAUL:

My wife has a difficult character. You will be my consolation.

PAULINE:

With passion! (knocking at the door) It's she! (Pauline pulls away)

PAUL:

You can never get any peace and quiet. Who's there?

VOICE:

(outside) The Cop.

PAULINE:

(with a sigh of relief) I prefer that.

PAUL:

(opening the door) Me, too.

COP:

You want me for something?

PAUL:

Yes, officer, but you arrived too late.

COP:

That's always the case. What happened?

PAUL:

Miss Pauline.

COP:

Hello, Miss Pauline.

PAULINE:

Hello, officer.

PAUL:

Miss Pauline came to get a bag of laundry. My wife was out. I was looking for the bag, when suddenly—

(The Cop sits down and lights his pipe.)

PAUL:

A woman of eighty years old entered—

COP:

Are you sure of her age?

PAUL:

Within a few years.

COP:

This isn't really serious.

PAUL:

Let me finish—

COP:

Have you got a light?

PAUL:

Here—

COP:

(lighting up) Thanks.

PAUL:

Then, this old woman, this old harpy, approached me, made incoherent remarks to me, threw herself at me, and insisted on "Conjugal caresses".

COP:

Case is solved. She's a madwoman.

PAUL:

She showed me her legs.

COP:

What for?

PAUL:

I have no idea! She seemed to be under the delusion they were attractive. Then she tried to kill us, Miss Pauline and me. I sent Miss Pauline to find you.

COP:

Did the right thing, 'cause with me, no time to waste.

PAUL:

I was forced to throw her out before you got here.

COP:

Under the circumstances, no need for a jury trial.

PAUL:

That's what happened.

COP:

And that's fine, fine, fine.

PAUL:

Fine? That's going a little far.

COP:

No use beating a dead horse.

PAUL:

(stiffly) I regret having needlessly disturbed you.

COP:

Oh, it doesn't disturb me. My shift is over for the day.

PAUL:

(uneasy) Completely?

COP:

Completely. Nothing more to do until after supper.

PAUL:

And when do you eat?

COP:

In two hours.

PAUL:

You dine late.

COP:

Oh, not really.

PAUL:

You don't go home to rest between your tours of duty, do you?

COP:

I prefer to go elsewhere. At home my wife is always scolding me a bit. I'm more at ease at the Donut Shoppe. (Pauline exchanges an anguished look with Paul)

COP:

See, I'm very content just to be here.

PAUL:

Me, too. I'm very happy to see you.

COP:

I want to ask you a question. Last week, I was paid a visit by your cousin.

PAUL:

He's a charming man.

COP:

Charming. He made me drink a whiskey. Really, a whiskey. I've never had anything like it. I wasn't sure how matters stood. Then he said: "You don't have to go a long way to get another one like it. My cousin, the Professor, has two good casks of it. Just a short way from you." He meant you, of course.

PAUL:

(excitedly) He's mistaken. I don't have a drop of alcohol in my house. My wife forbids me to drink.

COP:

In that case, you've probably got it hidden behind the woodpile.

PAUL:

I assure you, no, officer.

COP:

Still, your cousin—

PAUL:

My cousin drinks too much.

COP:

All the same he's a great guy, your cousin. He told me you also have some champagne.

PAUL:

But what made him tell you such things?

COP:

He couldn't have invented—

PAUL:

The alcohol was fermenting in his brain and confused him—

COP:

He carries his liquor very well. And his mind was sharp.

PAUL:

I don't understand a word, not a word of his insinuations.

PAULINE:

(worn out) Gentlemen, I bid you goodbye.

PAUL:

(desperate) Are you leaving, Miss Pauline?

PAULINE:

It's getting late. I'll return another day to square accounts.

PAUL:

(excitedly) Not at all! Not at all! I'm going to give you a bill. Come here, Miss Pauline. (leading her to a chair) Money is needed for commerce. (very low voice) Go quickly and give this twenty dollars to the beadle's boy and tell him to ring the alarm.

PAULINE:

Good idea. (aloud) Goodbye, sir. Goodbye, officer.

PAUL AND COP:

Goodbye, Miss Pauline.

(She leaves hurriedly.)

PAUL:

She's very sweet, this Miss Pauline.

COP:

Yeah, but she doesn't have a good reputation.

PAUL:

(starting) What are you saying?

COP:

It's funny.

PAUL:

(controlling himself) You find that funny?

COP:

That your cousin made such a mistake.

PAUL:

I thought you were talking about Miss Pauline.

COP:

No indeed. She's not an interesting person.

PAUL:

(anxiously) You think so?

COP:

I know what I know.

PAUL:

What do you know?

COP:

That you are hiding a whiskey still.

PAUL:

You have a one-track mind.

COP:

Not me. I tell myself, if I didn't have such a long way to go to get some great moonshine whiskey as good as your cousin's, my life would be—

PAUL:

You only think of moonshine whiskey.

COP:

(lugubrious) That can't be in question here anymore. (the alarm bell sounds) Must be a catastrophe!

PAUL:

There's a fire in town. Evidently it is a catastrophe.

COP:

(looking complacently towards heaven) I was talking about the moonshine whiskey. Which was only a hope.

PAUL:

You hear the alarm?

COP:

Are you sure it's the alarm?

PAUL:

You must be hard of hearing.

COP:

Me? Hard of hearing? Who can say that? I've got the trained ear of a police officer.

PAUL:

Then, what do you hear?

COP:

A bell.

PAUL:

It's the alarm bell, I tell you.

COP:

Sometimes that might be true, but with your stories about moonshine, I doubt it.

PAUL:

(solemnly) It's your duty.

COP:

(not budging) I'm going.

PAUL:

(exasperated) I've had enough of seeing you so calm! What is it all about? Are you really not going to rush to manage the conflagration?

COP:

(worried) Manage the conflagration?

PAUL:

You make me splutter with your tranquil air! You've got to go keep back the crowd of onlookers.

COP:

(rising, very annoyed) How can I keep back the crowd all by myself? And my shift is over already.

PAUL:

When duty calls, it's your duty to work after your shift is over.

COP:

Thanks for telling me my job. But it's tough all the same.

PAUL:

Go, officer, go.

COP:

I'm going, sir, I'm going. But with death in my heart.

(Paul slams the door behind him.)

PAUL:

Vanish, infamous slanderer, who gossips about the reputation of Pauline, who is purity itself 'cause she loves me! Go! Go! Run find whoever rang the false alarm. Use your flat feet to pursue the beadle's little boy who has twenty bucks in his pocket. I'd rather cut off my arms and legs than let you taste my moonshine. Moonshine that I am going to drink when my unbearable wife is out visiting or asleep. Ah! You interrupted the ravishing hugs of Pauline? Ah! You outstay your welcome? Ah! You wasted my time? Run, feet, after that beadle's boy. But you'll never catch him 'cause he's even faster than you are! (knocking) Is it you, Pauline? O joy! My wife is, as I know only too well, in the process of exposing her legs to the guests at her cousin's. (more knocking) But you, you are the adorable mystery of woman. The one that is unknown in detail. (opens the door)

(A superb Marine in dress uniform appears.)

MARINE:

Hello, Paul.

PAUL:

(astounded) You know me?

MARINE:

(entering with authority) Paul, don't play the fool!

PAUL:

Sir, I do not allow you—

MARINE:

Shut up! Take me in your arms and give me an interminable, languishing kiss!

PAUL:

(retreating behind the table) Sir, I have a horror of jokes that are in doubtful taste.

MARINE:

Listen, Paul. You've got to be reasonable.

PAUL:

You insinuate that I am mad? Return to your barracks and await my seconds!

MARINE:

Don't I look ravishing?

PAUL:

Evidently! Your uniform is very pretty! Anyway, I ask myself how you got here. There's no Marine base around here.

MARINE:

(brandishing his sword) Paul, if you continue, I am going to have you confined.

PAUL:

Will you please stop brandishing that dangerous weapon!

MARINE:

Are you speaking of my umbrella? There's something about it that distracts you today. Just now you were telling me that it was a cudgel. Now you say it's a sword.

PAUL:

(conciliatory) Listen, sir. We're all men here, and, between reasonable men, I dare hope that, despite your truly extravagant way of entering my house—

MARINE:

Since you are speaking more sedately, I am quite ready to forgive all your brutalities just now when you shoved me out the door.

PAUL:

I shoved you out the door?

MARINE:

Yes, to remain shut up with the laundress! That breaks my heart!

PAUL:

It's you who need to be confined! I don't understand how your commanding officer let you leave your camp! You are a public danger.

MARINE:

Paul, I am speaking to you calmly. Why do you say I am a Marine?

PAUL:

Because you are! Do you know what you are? Yes or no? This uniform, these boots, these braids—

MARINE:

I have braids? Me? You treat me like a Marine. But, it's less vexing than hearing myself called a witch, a vampire, or a monstrous octogenarian by you.

PAUL:

Now you pretend you are that old octogenarian witch? This is unheard of.

MARINE:

What witch? There's no witch! Just me! Me alone! Ah, Paul, Paul, look how pretty and well made my legs are.

PAUL:

Legs again? This is incomprehensible! The two sexes speak only of their legs, show only their legs. It's becoming a fashion nowadays.

MARINE:

Paul, I repeat to you what I said before. Come back to me!

PAUL:

(hand over his face) My head is spinning. Too much emotion for one day. I see witches and Marines whirling before my eyes.

(Pauline enters.)

MARINE:

(seeing Pauline, grabbing Paul) I've found you again, idol of my soul.

PAULINE:

(seeing Paul in the arms of a Marine) I feel ill. (she totters and falls into a faint)

PAUL:

(trying to escape) Pauline. Come to!

MARINE:

Don't bother about her! Now she's fainted, she'll leave us alone.

PAUL:

Before it was the Cop, now it's the Marine. There's a kind of fate preventing me from remaining alone with Pauline. It's revolting.

MARINE:

Don't call me a vampire any more. Or a witch or a Marine.

PAUL:

My head is boiling over.

(The Cop enters.)

MARINE:

(still grasping Paul) Give me that interminable, languishing kiss that I just asked for.

COP:

(dropping his night stick) For God's sake!

MARINE:

(loosening his grip) What's that noise?

COP:

I am speechless.

PAUL:

Officer, deliver me from this Homoerotic Horsemarine! The Marines have landed.

COP:

(sourly) He's no more a Marine than that was a fire. And the alarm was a false alarm.

PAUL:

There's something strange in all this!

MARINE:

Officer, you are a reasonable man. Understand me! My Paul is the victim of an illness as secret as it is horrible.

COP:

Who are you, sir?

MARINE:

The wife of my Paul.

COP:

What's this, sir? You, a man respected in the community—

PAUL:

I am going to confess everything to you.

COP:

(turning away his face) What am I going to hear?

PAUL:

It's a fact. I have a still.

COP:

I can breathe again.

PAUL:

Just now, besieged by an old fury, I sent for you. You came too late. But, by an extraordinarily rare piece of luck, you returned just as this Marine had the unheard of pretension to rape me. Rid me of this extravagant presence and I'll give you two little bottles of moonshine.

COP:

Agreed! Ha! My fine lad! You are dealing with high-class folks. (punching the Marine) I wasn't able to catch the prankster who rang the false alarm. But you, I've got you. And that will do. (dragging the struggling Marine to the door)

MARINE:

This is a scandal. I am in my own home and the police are putting me out!

COP:

I forbid you to bite me.

MARINE:

I am a martyr.

COP:

If you keep scratching my neck, I will kick you in the ass, my little friend!

MARINE:

I am going back to my cousin! And I will show my legs one more time. TO THE WHOLE COMPANY! IN FACT I'LL DO A STRIP TEASE. (punches the Cop and runs out)

COP:

(calmly) I'll catch him, Professor. Later. (noticing Pauline) Miss Pauline is asleep in the chair?

PAUL:

Don't you worry about Miss Pauline! I am going to wake her up. Run after the Marine and catch him.

COP:

No hurry.

PAUL:

Run, I say.

COP:

(more and more calm) Okay, I'll run. I'll return for those two little bottles. At your service. (picks up his truncheon and leaves)

PAUL:

Thanks from the bottom of my heart! Ah, darling Pauline. She hasn't come to. I'm going to take advantage so as to kiss her till I'm satisfied. (kissing her ardently) How convenient if the woman is unconscious. (continuing to kiss her) You can do whatever you like. Ah, what fine skin. It's delirious. It's exquisite.

PAULINE:

Not my neck. That makes me scream.

PAUL:

You're coming back to life. What joy!

PAULINE:

Ah, Paul, Paul.

PAUL:

Pauline.

PAULINE:

What must I think of you.

PAUL:

Appearances are against me, it's true.

PAULINE:

Really?

PAUL:

But my soul is pure.

PAULINE:

I'd like to believe it.

PAUL:

The Cop can be my witness. He threw out the Marine.

PAULINE:

(weeping) You are telling me lies. It's not possible that the cops came when they could be useful.

PAUL:

Don't feel bad! He came after you had fainted in such a touching way. Look, Pauline, you ought to realize the arrival of the Marine was not natural.

PAULINE:

That's what made me lose my senses.

PAUL:

(eagerly) Let's hope you'll find them, Pauline.

PAULINE:

That Marine was so handsome. And his uniform was so pretty. A military uniform has a certain effect. (knocking at the door)

PAUL:

(eyes to heaven) Oh. I can't have a private conversation, even for a minute, with the woman I love. I'm disgusted.

(The Marine enters.)

MARINE:

I came in since no one said, "Come in."

PAUL:

This is too much. The cop didn't collar you!

MARINE:

That cop is an alcoholic brute. He was looking for me while he was drinking. He didn't find me, so I've come back!

PAULINE:

Ah! He's a handsome Marine! (throwing herself at him and twining around him) This uniform, these boots, these braids, these tight pants.

MARINE:

Miss, will you please release me? What kind of manners are these? Is it because I wear tight pants?

PAULINE:

(grabbing him) Oh! He's irresistible.

PAUL:

(trying to pry Pauline off the Marine) Pauline, you are tearing my happiness to shreds.

MARINE:

This is nice! You see the effect that has! Yes, you can see the effect that has...when the person you love throws herself into the arms of another under your eyes. Well, that's what you did to me!

PAUL:

(trying to pull her to him) Pauline! I would never have believed this of you.

PAULINE:

(molesting the Marine) What do you want? I'm a woman.

PAUL:

That's not a reason.

PAULINE:

(still clutching the Marine) There are moments when you please me a lot. But this Marine! Ah, this Marine! How perfectly made he is!

MARINE:

(struggling) Little horror. Don't you have any shame? And what manners! To twine around a woman when you are one. That's scandalous!

PAULINE:

(still hugging) You stepped on the Moonshine Vine and you think you are a woman. That's not true! You are Mr. Perfect!

MARINE:

You are scratching my back. That hurts me. I'm going to whack you.

PAULINE:

(still hugging greedily) I prefer your whacks to anyone else's kisses. Whack me!

PAUL:

(in despair) Pauline!

MARINE:

I am avenged. Admire the fate of men who cheat. They are captivated by the first to come along. And she throws herself into the arms of the first to come along.

PAULINE:

(squeezing harder) Oh, you are naughty to say I am the first to come!

MARINE:

(getting loose) That's enough! Paul, remain with your laundress. You see what she wants! (she hurls Pauline into the arms of her Paul and flees)

PAUL:

(falling into a chair) Pauline, I am destroyed.

PAULINE:

(sitting in his lap) Me, too.

PAUL:

My sentimental life is over.

PAULINE:

Mine, too.

PAUL:

Let's cry together.

PAULINE:

Let's cry! But it's very sad to cry.

PAUL:

(lugubriously) The Cop was right. Your reputation isn't very good. There's no smoke without fire.

PAULINE:

Paul! That cop is a degenerate alcoholic. He speaks ill of everyone 'cause he's always drunk.

PAUL:

(lugubriously) My eyes don't deceive me.

PAULINE:

Paul. Listen to me.

PAUL:

No. You've caused me too much pain.

PAULINE:

The Marine is gone! Let's not talk about him anymore. He doesn't want me. That's a fact. But you remain to me. You must accept what fate gives you.

PAUL:

That's easy for you to say after you preferred the whacks of that Marine to my ardent kisses.

PAULINE:

Everything will be explained, believe me. This morning, through an inexplicable lack of prudence, I was picking strawberries in the woods. I must have stepped on the Moonshine Vine. And at the moment I saw the Marine, I wasn't myself. It was a passing distraction and very forgivable—truly.

PAUL:

Women are given to very suspicious explanations.

PAULINE:

You are always telling me that the Moonshine Vine is an old wives' tale. That's where you are wrong. Besides, it was only your wife I was pursuing with my attentions. So! Everything is straightened out.

PAUL:

Ah! You know how to get me. Pauline, you are a creature of charm and sweetness. Adorable creature, I will cure you of your naiveté with the aid of my scientific method. We are at peace here now. Yes, alone at last. Let's resume the course of our dear studies. Excuse me. I am always buried in studies so I employ that beautiful expression. Let's resume the course of our tender embraces.

PAULINE:

Very willingly.

PAUL:

Return to my arms.

PAULINE:

(leaping into his arms) Done!

PAUL:

You were saying— Not on the neck; it makes you scream.

PAULINE:

It's too much for me.

(The Cop enters.)

PAUL:

Now what?

COP:

(dropping his night stick) Oh!

PAUL AND PAULINE:

(moving apart) What?

COP:

Pay no attention! I'm so emotional.

PAULINE:

The emotion is ours!

COP:

Have no fear. I am a graveyard of secrets. I never tell what I know about people.

PAUL:

Hum! Hum!

COP:

Just like I'm telling you.

PAUL:

There's nothing to tell! I was showing Miss Pauline how that crazy Marine was behaving towards me.

COP:

Right! Right! I came to take delivery of those bottles of whiskey.

PAUL:

I'm going to get them.

COP:

You have some champagne, too. I really love champagne.

PAUL:

Two bottles of champagne for you!

COP:

Speaking of that Marine, he got away from me.

PAUL:

That's understandable. You stopped, I don't know how many times, to pick up your truncheon before pursuing him.

COP:

They told me he fled into the woods. And Hell! I didn't want to go there for fear of the Moonshine Vine.

PAULINE:

You see! The officer takes as iron truths the frightening powers of the Moonshine Vine. (something collides violently with the door)

PAUL:

Who's knocking like that? It must be the Marine! Happily, you are here, officer.

COP:

(picking up his truncheon) I'm here for the whiskey, but also to exercise my functions. (another collision)

PAUL:

The door's not going to withstand it.

(A threatening cow comes in.)

COW:

MOOO!

(The Cop, Paul, and Pauline all seek refuge behind the table.)

COW:

Paul! Paul! My adorable Paul!

PAUL:

Officer. Hit it with your truncheon.

COP:

(dropping his truncheon) A talking cow! Never in my life. It's an enchanted cow!

(The cow pursues them around the table.)

COW:

You are back with the laundress. This is infamous. I'm going to kill her and you, too.

PAUL:

She's going to gore us. Officer, go get the Butcher! He'll know what to do with her.

COW:

After wanting to kick me out, now you want to deliver me to the Butcher!

PAUL:

I am going to go with you. To help you find him.

COW:

(barring his way) You shall not leave! Paul, I forgive you.

(He seeks refuge behind the table.)

PAUL:

My head must be deranged.

COW:

Kiss me on the lips!

PAUL:

When will that butcher get here?

COW:

You don't want to kiss me on the lips?

PAUL:

She's foaming at the mouth!

COW:

Don't I have a pretty dress?

PAUL:

Yes, yes.

COW:

Look. See how languid my eyes are.

PAUL:

I'm having a flash. I feel I'm going to faint.

COW:

(lying down) Come lie beside me. It will be very comfortable.

PAUL:

I am drowning.

COW:

Look at my pretty legs.

PAUL:

Legs. The beasts, too.

COW:

I am your life's companion. I am the person that will shut your eyes! If you don't sleep with me, I'll choke you, and there will be no one to bury you.

PAUL:

This is horrible.

COP'S VOICE:

(outside) She just came in as if she owned the place.

BUTCHER'S VOICE:

These animals are full of nastiness.

(The Butcher enters, in his smock, followed by the Cop, who hides behind him, and Pauline, who hides behind the cop.)

BUTCHER:

Officer, you go probe her from behind. I am going to tie her horns with my chain. (the cow gets up erect) Yes, yes, old girl. I've known others like you. (the cow is on its feet, horns lowered) Are you ready, officer?

COP:

(not bravely) I am. (drops his truncheon)

COW:

Clumsy old fool!

BUTCHER:

Who spoke?

COW:

(advancing threateningly) Me! You assassin of innocent animals.

BUTCHER:

The cow!

COW:

(taking a step forward) For whom do you take me, you ill-mannered fellow?

BUTCHER:

A talking cow! Never seen that before.

COW:

(charging him) I'll teach you to try to stick me in the butt. I'm going to whip your ass. (goring the Butcher in his kidneys)

BUTCHER:

Yi! Yi! I've been gored.

(The cow chases the group out.)

COP:

I'm going to call headquarters for reinforcements.

COW:

I spit on your reinforcements!

COP, PAULINE, BUTCHER:

(outside) Help! Help! Help!

(Confused noises can be heard. Darkness falls.)

BLACKOUT

COW'S VOICE:

(in the distance) Paul! Paul! Paul! (a clock strikes three o'clock) Paul, it's three o'clock.

(The lights go up.)

(The Paul is dozing in his chair, head in his scribblings. His pretty wife appears in her beautiful dress.)

WIFE:

Paul! (shaking him)

PAUL:

Huh? What? Excuse me.

WIFE:

A man who spends his time sleeping is ridiculous!

PAUL:

My work tires me!

WIFE:

We should have left already. Go get properly dressed. My cousin is expecting us. It's her birthday today.

PAUL:

Birthday parties bore me.

WIFE:

You always scorn my family. But you are coming to my cousin's party.

PAUL:

It's going to interrupt my work.

WIFE:

You mean you want to sleep some more. This isn't an office, it's a dormitory. You are going to thicken your blood by going to sleep after lunch.

PAUL:

Might dream, too.

WIFE:

Go get dressed. I am going to buy some perfume to intoxicate my cousin's guests. You'll find me in the perfume shop. And hurry up! (she leaves)

PAUL:

The Moonshine Vine. Perhaps it's not a superstition. The Moonshine Vine. I must have stepped on it, since I made the mistake of marrying an unbearable wife!

CURTAIN

ABOUT THE AUTHOR

Frank J. Morlock has written and translated many plays since retiring from the legal profession in 1992. His translations have also appeared on Project Gutenberg, the Alexandre Dumas Père web page, Literature in the Age of Napoléon, Infinite Artistries.com, and Munsey's (formerly Blackmask). In 2006 he received an award from the North American Jules Verne Society for his translations of Verne's plays. He lives and works in México.

www.ingramcontent.com/pod-product-compliance
Lightning Source LLC
LaVergne TN
LVHW041616070426
835507LV00008B/281